I0113107

Democratic Transition in Anglophone West Africa

Democratic Transition in Anglophone West Africa

Jibrin Ibrahim

Monograph Series

The CODESRIA Monograph Series is published to stimulate debate, comments, and further research on the subjects covered. The Series will serve as a forum for works based on the findings of original research, which however are too long for academic journals but not long enough to be published as books, and which deserve to be accessible to the research community in Africa and elsewhere. Such works may be case studies, theoretical debates or both, but they incorporate significant findings, analyses, and critical evaluations of the current literature on the subjects in question.

Author

Jibrin Ibrahim directs the International Human Rights Law Group in Nigeria, which he joined from Ahmadu Bello University where he was Associate Professor of Political Science. His research interests are democratisation and the politics of transition, comparative federalism, religious and ethnic identities, and the crisis in social provisioning in Africa. He has edited and co-edited a number of books, among which are *Federalism and Decentralisation in Africa* (University of Fribourg, 1999), *Expanding Democratic Space in Nigeria* (CODESRIA, 1997) and *Democratisation Processes in Africa*, (CODESRIA, 1995).

Democratic Transition in Anglophone West Africa

© Council for the Development of Social Science
    Research in Africa 2003,
Avenue Cheikh Anta Diop Angle Canal IV, BP. 3304, Dakar, Senegal.
Web Site: http://www.codesria.org

CODESRIA gratefully acknowledges the Carnegie Corporation for supporting the project on Democratic Transitions in Africa. Views and opinions expressed in the work are those of the author.

Layout by Hadijatou Sy Sané

CODESRIA Monograph Series

ISBN: 2-86978-122-9

CODESRIA would like to express its gratitude to the Swedish Development Co-operation Agency (SIDA/SAREC), the International Development Research Centre (IDRC), OXFAM GB/I, the Mac Arthur Foundation, the Canergie Corporation, the Norwegian Ministry of Foreign Affairs, the Danish Agency for International Development (DANIDA), the French Ministry of Cooperation, the Ford Foundation, the United Nations Development Programme (UNDP), the Rockfeller Foundation, the Prince Claus Fund and the Government of Senegal for support of its research, publication and training activities.

Contents

Acknowledgments

As I am not a specialist on all but one of the five countries covered in this study, I have had to rely on the good counsel of friends and contacts who have provided me with information, on and insight into, the dynamics of democratic transition in Anglophone West Africa. On the Ghanaian situation, I have relied on the help of the following: Professor Joseph Ayee, Head, Department of Political Science, Legon; Professor E. Gyimah-Boadi, Department of Political Science, Legon; Dr Kwesi Jonah, Lecturer, Department of Political Science, Legon; Dr Kwame Karikari, Director, School of Communication Studies, Legon; Dr Yao Graham, Deputy Director, Integrated Social Development Centre and Co-ordinator, Third World Forum, Ghana; Dr Emmanuel Akwetey, Lecturer, Department of Political Science, University of Stockholm; Dr Amos Anyimadu, Lecturer, Department of Political Science, Legon; Felix Anebo, Lecturer, Department of Political Science, Legon; Chris Atim, former General Secretary of the June 4th Movement, member of the PNDC and co-ordinator of the defence committees; and Zaya Yeebo, former minister for Youth and Sports.

On the Gambia, I have benefited from the following: Dr Lenrie Peters who chaired the National Consultation Committee; Gabriel Roberts of the Independent Electoral Committee, Halifa Sallah of FOROYAA newspaper and an opposition political party activist; Marie Mendy, civil servant; Baba Jallow member of National Consultation Committee and journalist with the *Observer*; D. A. Jawo of the *Observer* newspaper; Baboucar Gaye of Citizen FM Radio; Ousainou Darboe, leader of the United Democratic Party; Dr Siga Jagne, Director-General of the Women's Bureau; Amie Joof-Soli, Chair of the National Women's Council; Pa Modu Faal, secretary-general of the Gambia Workers Confederation; Usman Sillah of *FOROYAA*; and Ebrima Sall of CODESRIA.

I am particularly grateful to the high-powered team of intellectuals who discussed the draft research report in Accra on the 17 and 18 of November 1999 and provided immense insight into how the study could be improved. They are the following: Dr Baffour Agyeman-Duah, Centre for Democracy and Development, Accra; Dr Emmanuel Anning of the Centre for Development Research, Copenhagen; Dr Amos Aniyandu, Department of Political Science, University of Legon; Dr Attahiru Jega, Department of Political Science, Bayero University, Kano; Professor Takyiwaa Manuh,

Institute of African Studies, University of Legon; Ms Wata Modad, National Women's Commission of Liberia, Monrovia; Dr. Funmi Olanisakin, Department of War Studies, King's College, London; Mr Halifa Sallah, Foroyaa Information Bureau, Banjul; and Ms Dzodzi Tsikata, Institute of Statistical, Social and Economic Research, University of Legon.

I have also received considerable assistance from CODESRIA staff, in particular, Mamadou Diouf who directed the research project and his collaborators, Ngone Diop Tine and Khady Sy.

1

Introduction

Africa has been undergoing an intense period of political conflict and transformation over the past decade. Central to this process of political reconstitution are the struggles aimed at combatting and reversing the continent's authoritarian past. These ongoing battles are intense, and there are continuous gains and reverses. In this paper, we set out to outline some of these changes. Our focus is Anglophone West Africa — Ghana, Nigeria, the Gambia, Sierra Leone and Liberia. What is the state of democratic transition in these countries? Have the struggles for entrenching political pluralism, civil and political rights and effective popular participation in the political process made significant and durable progress? Is there a regional political specificity characterising democratic transition in these five countries?

Democratic Transition

The notion of democratic transition implies a passage from a non-democratic to a democratic situation. In the context of this study, it is in essence a question that could only be posed in the long term because the establishment of a democratic system, however defined, would constitute a veritable transition only if it becomes a fairly permanent feature of political life. Diouf (1998) has outlined various arguments on the African debate relating to the question of whether the current situation on the continent should be considered, minimally, as mere political liberalisation, or, maximally, as genuine democratic transition. We believe that political liberalisation is part of the process of democratisation but the process itself can undergo reverses. The essential attributes of democratic transition include the following. At the formal level, there is the establishment of constitutional rule and the operation of a multiparty political system. At a more profound level the transition could be expected to involve socio-political transformation that allows freely elected rulers and the majority of the civil population to impose their supremacy over ruling oligarchies of the military or civilian ethno-regional cabals. This implies the development of a democratic political culture in which large sections of society internalise democratic values.

1

Citizenship participation must therefore be effective and it should result in genuine choice.

The most immediate challenge confronting the process of democratic transition presently taking place in Africa is that of ensuring that democratisation is accompanied by the institutionalisation of constitutional rule. Constitutions, it is generally acknowledged, do not in themselves make democracy. Indeed, many so-called democracies, especially in Africa, are not based on constitutional rule. Many of the alleged democratic transitions that have occurred in Africa have not led to constitutional rule and have therefore not crossed the first threshold that defines such a transformation. Most African constitutions are excellent documents, they have most of the right provisions about the rule of law, human, civil and political rights, elective institutions, governmental accountability, separation of powers etc. The problem however is that these provisions are not followed. Most African political systems are characterised by excessive arbitrariness and abuse of power, the lack of basic freedoms, and denial of popular sovereignty.

The year 1990 was an important threshold for democracy in Africa. Between 1990 and 1994, thirty-one of the forty-one countries that had not held multiparty elections did so (Diouf 1998:5). The transition has however not been smooth. At the empirical level, it is clear that the new wave of democratisation in Africa has not been progressing and stabilising as has been hoped. In countries such as Togo, Kenya, Gabon and the former Zaire, the authoritarian regimes manipulated democratic forms and remained in power. In other countries such as Niger, The Gambia and Sierra Leone, the military returned to power through coups-d'état. In Nigeria, elections that were to have produced an elected President were annulled in 1993, and transition did not occur until 1999. Only Botswana, Mauritius, Senegal and Zimbabwe have been able to sustain the independent democratic regimes that took over power after the retreat of colonialism. Even this achievement has been at the cost of the non-alternation of the ruling party, except in Mauritius.

One result of these setbacks is that a significant proportion of the African people have not yet had the opportunity to experience democracy. The bulk of the participants of the democratic experiments of the early 1960s, both the leaders and the followers, have faded away. The current generation of Africans is yet to engage fully with stable democratic politics. Indeed, the encounter of the current generation of Africans with politics is tainted with bitter images and memories of repression and authoritarianism. This is the political culture of which most Africans have had concrete experience.

Precisely because of this legacy of an authoritarian political culture, many African regimes have been shaken over the past two decades by agitations for democratic transitions. People see the need for a change in the quality of their political and social lives. Democratisation is on the African agenda because it has been denied to the people in such a systematic manner and for such a long time. Human rights are so urgently needed because the African person has been stripped of rights and dignity. All human beings who are subjected to the arbitrary powers of others sooner or later seek release and relief from them. They seek freedom, a need that arises out of the deprivation of liberty. Much of the recent history of the African people therefore revolves around intense struggles for freedom, for human rights and indeed for democracy. Even if success is limited, the struggle itself is profound. Democratic transition has not been easy because the stakes are very high. For the President's men, on the one hand, democratic transition represents the loss of power, privilege and the wealth that have been and is being accumulated from the state. For all those that have been excluded for power, on the other, the overwhelming majority, there is the promise of a better tomorrow. For both sides, the stakes are worthy of a major battle. Our contention is that in most African countries, the democratic movement is strong enough to impose its own agenda in the long run, in spite of strong ruling class opposition.

Anglophone West Africa

The theme of democratic transition is a very appropriate one for a comparative study of recent political developments in a region such as Anglophone West Africa. From this perspective it is possible to move beyond a mere juxtaposition of parallel studies of the different countries. What is involved here is both an identification of difference and specificity, and the analysis of those transversal issues that cut across territorial boundaries. Democratic transition is a promising point of departure because it involves profound changes which affect institutions, processes, values and culture. It is also a universal human phenomenon, and reacts to the same type of stimuli in different areas.

Our region of study is composed of only five of the fifteen countries of West Africa. They are Nigeria, Ghana, Sierra Leone, The Gambia and Liberia. The first four were British colonies, while the last began as a kind of American outpost in the region. The main regional specificity is the use of English as the official language of state. Interestingly enough, it is an issue that is not politically significant.[1] Otherwise, it is very difficult to discern any common institutional traits in the sub-region. Only The Gambia maintained the British Parliamentary system for any length of time. While Nigeria started with a federal system of government, the others had centralised administrations. Perhaps the single most important common trait in the region, politically speaking, has been the predominance of the military. It is no surprise that its frequent companion has been political violence. This combination is however not specific to our area of study. It is a much wider phenomenon encountered on the African continent, and elsewhere.

Our approach in this study will consist of identifying the political specificity of each state, but with a major focus on developments in Ghana. This country has asserted itself as a model for the region in recent years, and deserves our closer attention. The analysis that follows therefore incorporates elements of a specific case study, but it is one that we trust will be seen to be enriched by extensive consideration of related polities, and of the major transversal issues that criss-cross the region. These cross-regional issues, in the author's mind, are so significant that it is worth enumerating them right at the inception of the discussion, while accepting that other observers might come forward with somewhat altered concerns.

The Rise of a Militarised Security State

There has been a significant increase in the role of military and security forces in the political process of Anglophone West Africa. At the same time, the circulation of arms, private armed gangs and violence is very high. Political authority and legitimacy have declined and political entrepreneurs have been resorting increasingly to armed force, formal and informal, for accessing political power.

The Significant Increase in Public Corruption

The culture of public corruption initiated by earlier regimes has intensified in all the countries in the region. The activities of state actors, the military, security forces, international forces and armed gangs are increasingly being dictated by opportunities for corruption and accumulation.

An Intense Battle between Civil Society and the State

Political actors in civil society have become more active, and those in control of state power are engaged in desperate efforts to rein in and control these actors. The outcome of this struggle has strong implications for the consolidation of democracy.

The Appropriation of Gender Politics by the State:
The 'First Lady' or 'Bright Ladies' Syndrome

Gender politics has recently arrived at the centre stage of political life, but much of its dynamics is being appropriated and used by the wives and friends of the men in power. At the same time, by placing the gender question on the public agenda, new opportunities for gender equality struggles are being presented.

The Growing Disengagement Between Elections and Political Choice

Elections are organised frequently, but they do not usually lead to the installation of popular candidates in power. The electorate is often convinced that elections do not offer real political choices. At the same time, the struggle for free and fair elections has become the fulcrum of the struggle for democratic transition.

The Problematic of 'Democratic Transition' as a Negation of Genuine Democracy

There is growing political frustration in the region as the actors with arms increasingly adopt the rhetoric and tactics of a 'democratic transition' as a strategy for gaining and maintaining power. Powerful groupings have jumped on the bandwagon of democratisation, using popular discourses and manipulating public expectations in order to perpetuate their rule. Be that as it may, the fundamental problematic we need to engage with is whether or not programmes of 'democratic transition' lead towards the expansion of democratic space and democratic culture in spite of the intentions of the governing classes.

Coups d'état and the Ambitions of the Military: Salvation or Damnation

West Africa is one of the regions in the world that has been excessively marked by the high frequency of coups d'état and civil wars. Our analysis cannot but place heavy emphasis on the ways in which militarism has affected the possibilities of democratic transition. The military have been at the centre of power in the region over the past two decades. Presently, the Presidents of Benin, Burkina Faso, Côte d'Ivoire, Ghana, the Gambia, Niger, Nigeria, Guinea-Conakry, Guinea-Bissau and Togo are all serving or former military officers. Certain authors such as Harbeson (1987:2) have questioned the assumption that African military regimes are distinct and distinguishable from civilian regimes. He argues correctly that many civilian regimes in the continent are as authoritarian and hierarchical as military regimes. This argument is however short-sighted. While civilian regimes are indeed frequently authoritarian, their authoritarianism often functions as a tactical instrument rather than a worldview or value orientation. Military regimes are not only authoritarian in a structural sense, but also in their values and their politics. Their personnel are bred in a sub-culture that believes power can be wielded and conserved on the basis of the force that resides within the military institution itself. This is a value system that is committed to the destruction of politics as a benign mixture of bargaining, negotiating, force

5

and compromise. These values notwithstanding, military culture in Africa has generally led to the decomposition of political processes. Ultimately, the result is the antithesis of the military dream of the forceful imposition of order. Witnesses to this fact are the anarchic situations in Somalia, Liberia, Rwanda, to name but a few.

The most significant characteristic of political life in Anglophone West Africa in the 1990s was the move by military regimes to turn 'democratisation' and 'elections' into instruments for perpetuating their rule. In Liberia, Master Sergeant Doe carried out a coup against the ruling True Whig Party in 1980, massacred their top Americo-Liberian leadership and settled down to tyrannical rule. He instituted a regime of terror that eventually consumed him. Doe organised elections in order to enable him to continue in power. The only way to remove him was through armed conflict and a long and terrible civil war, carried out at great costs to the Liberian people. In Ghana, Jerry Rawlings was able to remain in power since his 'second coming' in 1981. He showed exceptional mastery of both the uses of violence as well as civilian political manipulation. Rawlings won two elections, and more importantly was the first to elaborate extensive political reforms aimed at disenfranchising established political parties and creating a playing field tilted in his favour. In Sierra Leone, yet another coup took place in 1992 bringing a young 'militariat' administration to power. They started with a programme of democratisation and reconstruction of institutions and ended up trying to perpetuate their own regime. Confronted with resistance by civil society and competing armed soldiers and groups, a ballet of changes in regimes have been occurring with the control of arms remaining the central issue. In the Gambia, another young member of the militariat organised a coup in 1994 and promised to hand-over power after a four-year transition. After being pressured into reducing the transition period to two years, he declared himself a candidate for the election and continued in power as a 'democratically' elected President. In Nigeria, the military have been organising numerous programmes of transition to democratic rule since 1985. After thirteen years of transition, the third military ruler in the recently concluded transition period, General Abdulsalam Abubakar, eventually organised elections and handed over power to an elected administration. This was a promise his two military predecessors had failed to keep. Very clearly, the politics of the military have proved an immense force in shaping and misshapen political systems throughout the region.

The impact of militarism on the political process of Anglophone West African is of such a kind that states often seem to be in transition or transformation to police states. All the regimes have invested heavily in the armed and security forces. Parallel security organisations have been established and the political leadership is convinced that its power base consists of these institutions, and not the people. Like Oliver Cromwell, their political line seems to be that 'Nine citizens out of ten hate me. What does it matter if the tenth alone is armed?' Militarism has led to a decline of institutions, the erosion of civil relations and the steady rise of violence in society. Indeed, military regimes in West Africa have succeeded in permeating civil society with their values — both the formal military values of centralisation and authoritarianism, and the coarse attitudes associated with 'barrack culture', hedonism and brutality that were derived from the colonial army. They are producing

> A lumpen culture that is textured by ignorance, political thuggery, hooliganism, banditry and warlordism. The devalorisation of humanity within the lumpen 'life world' is frequently displaced into the public domain when the militariat takes charge of the state (Kandeh 1996:388).

An important dimension of the new political tendency is the capture of state power by conspiratorial elements of the military underclass (private to lieutenant) — the 'militariat'. These putschists are young, with little education, and they take over power on an anti-corruption ticket. But they become very corrupt themselves. Their human rights record on the whole can only be considered abysmal (Kandeh 1996:395). They therefore never succeed in turning their populist coups into populist regimes.

Militarism is however not the only phenomenon in the sub-region. The basic outcome of decades of militarism has become manifest: the decomposition of state and society. One of the effects of this trend is the widespread growth of private armies and armed bands. The military is losing or has lost control of the means of violence in many of the countries. Numerous warlords with a stake in war have entrenched themselves and are fighting for the control of power and natural resources. The people have been forced to confront these elements which use arms recklessly and irresponsibly. The decomposition of state and society has demonstrated throughout the sub-region that for a brighter tomorrow, the influence of the military and armed groups on the polity must be curtailed, and political society and civil society must lead the struggle for an expanding democratic space. Democratic forces have therefore undertaken this fight-back, and are indeed succeeding in imposing their agenda on the future of society. It makes sense to speak of an ongoing process of democratic transition. In demonstrating this paradoxical development, we shall rely mainly on what we call the Ghanaian model.

2

The Ghanaian Model

Introduction

Ghana has been one of the African states that has been pursuing structural adjustment programmes since the early 1980s. The country is considered to be one of the 'good examples' of successful economic reform by the International Monetary Fund and the World Bank, although many observers believe that this 'success' is exaggerated (Parfitt 1995:55; Green 1995:581). It is also considered one of the countries that has made a successful transition from military rule to democratic governance, albeit with the incumbent military ruler transforming himself into a civilian politician and President.[2] It is an example that has been followed by General Momoh of Sierra Leone, Colonel Yahya Jammeh of the Gambia, and was attempted by the late General Abacha of Nigeria, until his sudden death in June 1998. Outside our area of focus, other examples in West Africa are Blaise Compaore of Burkina Faso, and Baré Mainasara of Niger, who was assassinated on 9 April 1999.

The Ghanaian model consists of the ability to transform an authoritarian militarised state into a legitimate one. It is the opposite of what one could call the Liberian model of militarisation, generalised brutality, civil war, arbitrary rule and virtual anarchy. The Ghanaian model is about the reinstatement of institutions, the rule of law, pluralist elections, press freedom, effective local government and public probity in a state that has suffered considerable decay. It is therefore a model about the gradual improvement of state efficacy, democratic governance and respect for human rights. The explication of this Model requires reference to the remarkable success of the Ghanaian President, Jerry Rawlings, who has entered the literature as yet another charismatic redeemer on the continent.

Rawlings, the State and the End of Charisma and Redemption

Ghana's first President, Kwame Nkrumah, has been portrayed as one of Africa's leading charismatic figures. Many of the foremost political scientists of the 1960s — Austin, Ake, Apter and Mazrui — devoted considerable

8

attention to Nkrumah's charismatic authority and its limits (Assimeng 1986:158). As is well known, Nkrumah's bright leadership qualities did not last for long as repression and crisis developed in the mid-1960s, ultimately leading to his overthrow in 1966. In the 1980s, a new round of debate started on charisma and redemption, this time as represented in the person of a young military officer, Jerry Rawlings. Many scholars have posed the question about whether Rawlings's relative success is linked to his charismatic attributes. It is worthwhile therefore to briefly review the importance and limits of charisma.

The lowest point in Ghana's political development was undoubtedly the Acheampong regime of 1972-1978. Acheampong had replaced the elected government of Busia, which was accused of corruption and mismanagement. The Acheampong regime, however, turned out to be even more corrupt than the preceding ones. In July 1978, a palace coup by General Akuffo led to the removal of General Acheampong. The ban on politics was lifted and a Constituent Assembly was put in place. But there was no serious punishment instituted against the corruption and abuse of office of the previous regime. On May 5th, 1979, an attempted coup by Jerry John Rawlings occurred. It was foiled and Rawlings suffered detention. On June 4th, 1979, he was rescued from jail by the junior ranks of the armed forces and he took over power in a 'spontaneous revolution'. The coup makers defined their political objective as establishing justice before elections and before a hand-over to a civilian regime.

When Rawlings assumed power, the economic crisis had reached catastrophic levels. The intake of calories per capita for example was only 68 percent of the minimum required (Sandbrook and Oelbaum 1997:612). The Ghanaian people desperately needed a redeemer and Rawlings played that role because he was considered to be a man of the people (Verlet 1997:43). Rawlings initiated a crusade for moral discipline, for probity in social and economic life and for accountability. The essential ingredient of Rawlings's initial charisma was his insistence that no persons were too big or too small to be punished for their faults. The initial targets of the corrective punitive measures were senior military officers and their civilian collaborators. The circle however quickly widened to include smugglers, hoarders, tax defaulters, lodge members and so on. These policies seemed to represent a profound critique of the existing social structure and a cry for transformation. On this basis arose perceptions of the charismatic leadership of Rawlings himself. That charisma, however, had a thin veneer that covered a reign of terror. 'It embodied the type of terror to end all terrors, because the circumstances that called for such terror were going to be eliminated' (Assimeng 1986:152).

Kwame Karikari (1998) reminds us that Nkrumah's worst breach of civil rights was the institution of detention without trial. But under Rawlings, Ghana saw the liberal use of the death penalty and frequent incidents of extrajudicial killing amounting to the terrorisation of the population. The Worker's Defence Committees and People's Defence Committees '[w]rought havoc on peaceful citizens. They beat up people who would not bend to their obtuse and perverse and misguided wishes and harassed people. They took the law into their own hands, arrested people, tried them and imposed senseless fines on them' (Ansah 1996:88). Ansah adds that there was a hit list of people to be permanently silenced.

In April 1993, the government introduced a structural adjustment programme (SAP). It soon became clear that the end of suffering was not in sight, and Rawlings's alleged charisma underwent a steep decline:

> Charisma, as in the case of messianism appears to follow the law of diminishing marginal utility. The longer its persistence, the more attenuated its long-term charm in the minds and hearts of even its closest followers… [Rawlings's] charismatic stance is analogous to that of messianic movements as a whole, and the reality of unfulfilled promises sooner or later catches up with such a stance (Assimeng 1986:156).

Rawlings's response to the opposition that mounted against his harsh economic policies was to increase the level of repression through his network of security personnel. In this regard it is worth noting that Rawlings's original coup had not been a classic military one (Gymah-Boadi 1998). The core military establishment had not been involved. No generals served as ministers or heads of parastatals. It was therefore more of a paramilitary coup. At the same time, Rawlings was very security conscious and had built up a vast personal security system.

Nevertheless, the figure of Rawlings himself requires deeper study. His populist stance brought him much popular support, and he has been a central actor in the remoulding of the Ghanaian state. The specificity of the current Ghanaian path to democratic transition has been generally subsumed into what is called the 'Rawlings Factor'. West Africa has of course been a very fertile ground for military populism. Besides Rawlings himself, other notable examples include Murtala Mohammed in Nigeria, Thomas Sankara in the then Upper Volta, and Samuel Doe in Liberia. Military populism has usually been generally accepted by the population in periods of critical political crisis in West Africa. The reason for this acceptance is that many people welcomed them as short-term corrective interventions. In a letter to Jerry Rawlings warning him not to contest in the 1992 General Elections for example, one of his ministers of the 1982–84 period argued that 'My serious study of the political scene, over the past two years, has convinced me that Jerry Rawlings, like Moses, was for short-term deliverance only. He is NOT for leadership to the promised land (Dake 1992:10, Emphasis in the original).

The 'promised land' referred to here is the vision of a stable and democratic Ghana. Dake contended that Rawlings's military training and background disqualified him from long-term democratic stewardship. Since then, Rawlings has served two full terms as an elected president and did not try to change the constitution to contest during the 2000 elections.

The Rawlings factor means different things to different people. One aspect is his popularity throughout the region. This popularity is linked to the dramatic manner in which he entered the political scene, which has been outlined above. According to Shillington, in his book *Ghana and the Rawlings Factor*, some people dismiss the Ghanaian leader's accession to power as that of an amoral, drug-crazed womaniser, who also practices voodoo. More commonly however, people have perceived the Rawlings Factor as signalling the emergence of the first Ghanaian leader since Nkrumah to be imbued with charisma. He is also often praised for his ability in leading Ghana through years of economic recovery and giving Ghanaians back their national pride and self respect (Shillington 1992:131).

One of the closest collaborators of Rawlings in his early days in power and a member of the PNDC, Chris Atim (1998), argues that the impact of Rawlings was due to the fact that he was not just interested in gaining political power or looting the treasury. Rawlings's main concern 'was to change people's lives in a positive manner'. The Rawlings regime was very repressive during the initial period but later toned down its harshness, realising that force would not work in the long run. Chris Atim believes that although Rawlings himself could truly be considered charismatic, the latter was very distrustful of the idea, having seen how Nkrumah fell from power despite his immense prestige in Africa. Instead, Rawlings's strategy was to depend on producing results. No wonder, adds Atim, that Rawlings could separate Brong Ahafo from Ashanti, destabilise Nkrumah's political base, genuinely convert to the ideology of the IMF, and successfully neutralise the army.

Kwame Karikari (1998) describes the Rawlings factor as consisting of the ability to maintain antagonistic social strands together around his personality. While Rawlings represents the comprador class, he still appeals to the petty bourgeoisie and the lumpen. Rawlings has taken structural adjustment to its extreme limits — sold off national assets, promoted foreign businesses against the interests of the national bourgeoisie, and brought back the Levantines. At the same time, however, he has kept the middle class happy by providing opportunities for consultancies and projects. Karikari believes that, politically, Rawlings represents a regression from real political independence and the undermining of national self respect and dignity, including subservience and obsequiousness to whites in general. It is not surprising that 'Whites Only' Clubs are returning to the scene.

In contrast, Amos Anyimadu (1998) has defined the Rawlings factor as the ability to re-launch radical populism in Ghanaian politics — bringing the famed 'veranda boys' back in. It is a feat that the Nkrumahists have been unable to re-enact. Rawlings was able to bring a new perspective to leadership by showing that even the biggest can be made to pay for their sins. He adds that it is more than style. It is also a question of governmentality.

At a different level of analysis, Chris Atim (1998) has argued that the binary nature of Ghana's politics — essentially coming down to the Ashanti versus the rest — has not changed, but that one of Rawlings's achievements has been to modernise Ghanaian politics by making the Nkrumahist agenda historically irrelevant. In a related vein, Yao Graham (1998) also suggests that Rawlings is not really the third force in Ghanaian politics he is reputed to be, although he has been able to incorporate militants from both the Ashanti and non-Ashanti camps. He considers that the two groupings remain powerful forces. For Joseph Ayee (1998) however, the Rawlings factor is the creation of a third force, a new dominant element in Ghanaian politics. Rawlings established himself unquestionably with the 1996 elections, which he clearly won. Ayee asserts that Ghanaians like Rawlings because he is colourful, he is not corrupt (although his ministers might be), he is youthful and he is able to get basic utilities such as electricity, water and schools to function. In addition, he has come out convincingly to identify with the people during periods of national emergencies.

For Gyimah-Boadi (1998), Rawlings's diverse ancestry has played a role. People see him positively as a 'White man' who is with the masses. People are impressed when he gets into the gutter to help workers clearing dirt. Given his positive image, his numerous *faux pas* are easily forgiven, as people's attitude is that 'he does not understand — he is not from here'.

The Ghanaian model is about a success-story — putting a moribund economy back to work and on the path of development. A World Bank study has contended that by the year 2020, Ghana will be as advanced as the Asian Tigers. Rawlings would be seen as the main architect of this success (Verlet 1997:35). Moving the polity from military dictatorship to a liberal democracy with two successful elections is the other facet of the success. In addition to the above, Rawlings has succeeded in maintaining himself in power for eighteen years. In the early period, the Rawlings regime evoked considerable internal and external antipathies. Over time however, Rawlings has been able to civilianise and civilise the regime, thus reducing the level of dislike to manageable proportions.

Kwesi Jonah (1998) contends that the usual arguments about Rawlings's success-story are faulty. Instead of constituting an economic success-story, the country is suffering from excessive inflation, an energy crisis, a balance of payments crisis and so on. Most of Rawlings's achievements in terms of infrastructure and services are in urban Ghana — Accra and Kumasi — where the World Bank has pumped a great deal of resources to paint a pretty picture for the world. Rawlings, he argues, has done little for rural Ghana. Paradoxically, urban Ghana has consistently voted against Rawlings while rural Ghana has consistently voted for him. Jonah argues that while there is indeed a Rawlings success-story, it is not rooted in what he has done. Rather, it is rooted in what he is — someone who has an image of a man of the people, a helper of the oppressed, a kind ear. Rural Ghana still has that image of Rawlings, the urban dwellers no longer have faith in his charismatic endowments. Although as Jonah argues, we must not exaggerate the Rawlings regime's contribution to rural Ghana, many observers point out that a number of externally financed water and electricity projects have been carried out in the rural areas, and Rawlings of course takes credit for the work done. Another dimension of Rawlings's success over the past fifteen years is that he has been able to convince Ghanaians that the era of the welfare state is over and that people have to fend for themselves. With the growth of the self-help ideology, people do not expect much from Government anymore and they do not therefore blame the state for non-performance in social provisioning.

Corruption

The emergence of Rawlings on the Ghanaian political scene was grounded in the anti-corruption struggle. The height of corruption in Ghana was during the Acheampong regime, which was overthrown a year before Rawlings first appeared on the scene. Rawlings focussed his energies in the fight against corruption not just within the state but also in civil society. In June 1979, the regime demolished Makola market in Accra on the grounds that it was a den of *Kalabule* (corruption). Market women in particular, were accused of profiteering and of being the enemies of the people (Munah 1993:180). Many market women were harassed, flogged in public and humiliated, allegedly for profiteering. The Rawlings regime threw 20,000 women out of the market in

Accra (Tsikata 1997:398). At the level of the state, revolutionary justice was applied to top military officers and members of the administrative cadre and political class who had been found to be corrupt.

Rawlings's charisma and populism have flowed into the corruption debate. So many Ghanaians assert that Rawlings is not corrupt, even if his ministers are, and his wife may be too. Far too many people are ready to give him the benefit of the doubt. The general assumption is that he is more interested in power and in glory, than in material acquisition. There are however persistent rumours about his corruption. From the Nigerian end, for example, there are allegations that he has been receiving regular supplies of crude oil from the Nigerian government and pocketing the proceeds. Secondly, after the death of Abacha, it was revealed that there were records indicating that $5 million was given to Rawlings for image laundering of the Abacha regime (*Guardian* 29/30/1999). According to Amos Anyimadu, Rawlings over the years has regularly revisited the anti-corruption theme in his speeches but has not been able to deal with all but a few of the corrupt politicians in his entourage.

Corruption remains a major problem under the Rawlings regime. A major attitudinal survey carried out by the Centre for Democracy and Development (1999:34) in Accra revealed that official corruption was still a major problem in Ghana. Nearly 85 percent of Ghanaians thought that bribery was common among public officials while 76 percent of the population thought that most government officials and politicians were mainly concerned about enriching themselves. In fact, barely 63 percent of the population thought that official corruption was now worse than under the old military regime. The clear conclusion from the study is that in spite of Rawlings tough rhetoric against corruption, not much has changed in that domain.

Civil Society

Ghana's civil society has played an important role in the struggle for democracy. Civil associations and professional groups have been deeply involved in the struggle for democracy (Amankwah 1996:130). When Acheampong tried to impose Union Government in 1977 for example, the Ghana Bar Association and other sectors of the Ghanaian elite came out and fought against it and demanded a multiparty liberal democratic model (Jonah 1987). In fact, as has been argued:

> The Ghana Bar Association has always fought against oppressive and dictatorial regimes which have abounded in this country for nearly forty years. During the first republic, it was the late J.B. Danquah, one-time

president of the Ghana Bar Association, who fought relentlessly against oppressive rule and particularly against the use to which the Preventive Detention Act was put (Adjetey 1996:72).

There is a long history of teacher activism in Ghana, which has been traced to the period of the depression in the 1930s. Although largely non-political, teacher activism has helped empower Ghanaian civil society (Nyoagbe 1996:79). The Association of Recognised Professional Bodies (ARPB), however, has been very politically active since its inception in 1977. This organisation came out openly to organise a strike in opposition to Acheampong's Union Government plans (Okudzeto 1996:109). The ARPB was also very critical of the Rawlings regime. Between 1983 and 1985, the government under Rawlings arrested and detained many executive members of the organisation and it was not until 1991 that the organisation was allowed to resume its activities (Okudzeto 1996:128).

The strength of Ghana's civil society should not be exaggerated. As Ninsin (1993a:17) has argued, civil society is rooted in the middle class, and in Ghana it is a small one. Furthermore, those active in both professional organisations and political activity have been very few. Another problem is that much of the space of Ghana's 'civil society' is occupied by religious movements whose strength seems to have grown as rapidly as the strength of the students, workers and professionals movements has declined. Rawlings has also been very successful at crippling much of the country's civil society. Kwame Karikari argues that Nana Rawlings's '31st December Movement' has forcibly incorporated autonomous women's organisations and also monopolised all sources of foreign funding. The NDC has also absorbed youth organisations has weakened the student's movement.

As has been argued by Drah (1993:107), Ghanaian civil society has alternated precariously between contraction and expansion ever since independence. What is important, however, is that:

> Despite its vicissitudes, no dictatorship has succeeded in decreeing civil society out of existence. For some vital segments of civil society, like the Bar Association, Catholics Bishops Conference, Christian Council of Ghana, NUGS (in the greater part of its existence), University Teachers Association of Ghana, Registered Nurses Association, Medical Association, Traders' Association and so on, have over the years evolved a liberal culture of resistance to state interference in their affairs.

It is this liberal culture, entrenched over the years, that has made the country's civil society a constant ally in the struggle for enhancing democracy.

Gender and Democratic Transition: First Ladyship and the Birth of Democracy

One of the basic features of African society is the systematic discrimination against women. The question of redressing gender imbalance in the continent is therefore at the heart of the question of democratic transition. Tackie (1996:43) draws our attention to the fact that there are three main areas in which women are excluded in contemporary society: the military, religious organisations, and politics. In the Anglophone West African region we are considering here, the military have played a major role in society and politics and religion is becoming one of the most important elements in people's lives. In this context, therefore, the problem of promoting more equitable gender relations has become very problematic. In a sense, the spirit of militarism and patriarchal religious attitudes have combined to produce spectacular, personalised and authoritarian paths to resolving the gender question.

One of the most important aspects of the Ghanaian model has been the prominent role played by Jerry Rawlings's wife, Nana Agyeman-Rawlings, in creating a powerful and autonomous space for herself in the gender politics of the state. This phenomenon has been christened 'femocracy'. According to Amina Mama, femocracy is:

> An anti-democratic female power structure which claims to exist for the advancement of ordinary women, but is unable to do so because it is dominated by a small clique of women whose authority derives from their being married to powerful men, rather than from any actions or ideas of their own (Mama 1997:81).

Femocracies, Mama adds, exploit the commitments of the international movement towards greater gender equality in the interests of a small female elite. In so doing, they end up upholding the patriarchal system in society. After all, the basic assumption of the femocrats is that they should enjoy power because their husbands are in leadership positions (Tsikata 1998). The basic institutional framework around which femocracy is organised is the office of the First Lady.

From antiquity, certain wives of princes, monarchs and so on are known to have played significant roles in national and international politics. The 'First Lady Syndrome', in the sense in which we use it here, however, is a new international political phenomenon. It has been traced to the 1992 World Summit for the Economic Advancement of Rural Women hosted in Geneva at the initiative of six First Ladies, three of whom — Maryam Babangida, Elizabeth Diouf and Suzanne Moubarak — were African (Sage 1998:60-61). For the first time, wives of Heads of States sought to play an autonomous and co-ordinated role in international politics in their capacities as wives. For

16

Elizabeth Diouf for example, it was the first time she made a public speech on an international political platform. The First Lady Syndrome hit the international limelight in the 1995 Beijing Conference when a large group of First Ladies met in the context of a major world event and took the limelight. Hilary Clinton, wife of the American President and an illustrious person in her own right played a leading role.[3]

In Africa, the First Ladies Summit, was first hosted at Yaounde in Cameroon by President Paul Biya's wife, Chantal Biya, during the 1996 OAU Summit. In attendance were the wives of the Heads of the following states — Botswana, Burundi, Cape Verde, Cameroon, Congo, Gabon, Malawi, Namibia, Senegal, Sierra Leone and Tanzania (Sage 1998:61). The communiqué of the meeting, which focussed on strategies to improve the lives of rural women, was incorporated into the official communiqué of the OAU Meeting (Sage 1998:51). In July 1996, Mariam Abacha hosted ECOWAS First Ladies during the Abuja Meeting. In May 1997, Mariam Abacha hosted the first autonomous First Ladies Summit in Abuja, convened to contribute to peace building in Africa.

There is a basic problem with the First Lady syndrome. As one writer has argued, 'Even if the stance being taken by the First Ladies makes them role models for other women, the basis of their power promotes the idea that women can exercise authority or be considered successful and worthy of respect only if they marry well' (Tsikata 1998).

One author claims that one of the negative effects of the First Lady Syndrome is that it has increased the premium on good matrimonial strategies in contemporary Africa (Sage 1998). The First Lady Syndrome has been observed in Africa for some time. In the 1960s for example, the wives of Jomo Kenyatta in Kenya and Hamani Diori in Niger wielded a great deal of public influence and accumulated vast personal fortunes (Mama 1997:81 and Sage 1998).

Nana Rawlings is however the first person to systematically pursue the femocratic line on an organisational platform in Africa. She has no official position in government but has played a major role in formulating and even implementing policies relating to women.[4] The main organisational structure that she developed is the 31st December Women's Movement (DWM), named after the second coming to power of her husband in 1981. The DWM was officially launched on 15 May 1982. The DWM is a huge organisation with about thirty affiliate organisations and claims a membership of more than two million rooted in the countryside. The size of its membership is contested but it is certainly very high. The identity of the DWM has been shifting, from a women's political organisation, through a revolutionary organ to a non-governmental organisation (Tsikata 1998). It appears that the DWM was reconverted to an NGO so that it could benefit from grants for NGOs distributed by international funding agencies (Sandbrook and Oelbaum 1997:623). In spite of its conversion, some of its staff are still on the government payroll. It is also represented in the District Assemblies. The DWM has focussed on mobilising women for small-scale, village-level economic projects financed essentially from external grants. Indeed, what Nana Rawlings has done is to try to cover the space of women's organisations in Ghana by claiming to stand for all Ghanaian women while at the same time she has developed the DWM into a very partisan organisation at the service of her husband. The DWM has been used as an effective campaign instrument for Nana's husband's party, the NDC, during the 1992 and 1996 elections.

Nana Rawlings led the Ghanaian delegation to Beijing and has been presiding over the implementation of the post-Beijing decisions. Her style has completely personalised the pursuit of gender policies. For example, she has appointed a committee to draw-up affirmative action policies and handed out directives to the National Council of Women and Development (NCWD). Indeed, the NCWD has effectively been taken over by the DWM (Tsikata 1997:401). Nana Rawlings has succeeded in using the DWM to integrate women's organisations into the corporatist power structure of the NDC (Munah 1993:189).

Rawlings's wife has been so active on the political scene that there are rumours that she has presidential ambitions. Sakyi-Addo painted an interesting possible scenario for the year 2000, although in the event it did not come to pass:

> She will be Africa's first woman president. And there are many more firsts besides. After the oath is taken, the outgoing president hands the new president the scroll of office. They hug and kiss deeply on the mouth. There are a few catcalls. And then they simply swap seats: the First Lady is now the president and the president after 19 years in power becomes the First Gentleman: The first First Couple ever to switch roles (Sakyi-Addo 1998:20).

The importance of Nana Rawlings consists in being one of the leading precursors of the phenomenon of the 'First Lady' in demanding an important role for women in society. She was able to appropriate concerns that are current in the international development community about the necessity of focussing on rural and poor women. She virtually 'invented' rural women as an important constituency that all public officials in Ghana must pretend to identify with. She has also demonstrated that there is much money and influence to be gained in making claims to represent the women's movement, a phenomenon that is widely recognised today.

18

The gains for women produced by the Nana Rawlings phenomenon are marginal ones. A major study on the role of women in Ghanaian public life published in 1998 by the National Council on Women and Development, the Institute of Statistical, Social and Economic Research and the Ghana Institute of Management and Public Administration showed that:

> In almost all the institutions studied, there are signs of discriminatory practices ranging from the lack of transparency in promotions to maternity leave... Women in Parliament are yet to overcome their subordinate position in politics and their disadvantages... NGOs and religious humanitarian organisations are found to be as gender insensitive as central government institutions (*Public Agenda* 23 February 1998).

But the transformation of gender relations is a long-term project, and at least, it can be claimed that Nana Rawlings has put it on the public agenda.

Elections Without Choice: The Stolen Verdict

In 1992, the PNDC successfully transformed itself into the civilian regime of the NDC with Rawlings as the President. It was an 'undemocratic transition' (Ninsin 1993:10). The PNDC had monopolised political space and prevented other parties from operating freely. The regime refused even to open dialogue with other political forces. The state maintained all the repressive PNDC laws that had been enacted, appointed all the members of the electoral committee, and exercised a tight control over the mass media. As a leading Ghanaian political scientist put it, Ghana has a long tradition of civilian and military authoritarianism and the so-called 1992 transition was just another 'transition without change' (Gymah-Boadi 1994:78). Although a Commonwealth Observer Team had pronounced the 1992 presidential election 'free and fair', many observers were of the view that they were seriously flawed. Indeed, the New Patriotic Party issued a report containing detailed allegations of irregularities in 100 of the country's 200 constituencies. The Report was very influential and was entitled 'The Stolen Verdict: Ghana November 1992 Presidential Election'. The opposition political parties therefore decided to boycott the parliamentary elections as a form of protest against this 'stolen verdict'.

Another important factor concerning the 1992 elections were persistent reports that Rawlings had imported a great amount of weapons, 'which PNDC thugs, commandos and other ragamuffins were going to use to destabilise the country in case the NDC lost. Thank God, through means, foul or fair, J. J. Rawlings won and the thugs were denied the opportunity to be of service to their patron and master' (Ansah 1996). Indeed, it appears that many people decided to vote for Rawlings in order to allow him his two terms in

19

office and then depart in peace, rather than refuse him the popular mandate and have him stay by force and at a very high social and political cost.

Not all agree with this analysis. Chris Atim, for example, considers that the verdict was not really stolen and that Rawlings was sufficiently popular to have won the elections. He adds that the NPP were simply too arrogant to have admitted to losing the elections (Atim 1998). Another factor that influenced the election and which has parallels with other countries in the region was the idea of voting for peace. As Felix Anebo (1998) argues, it is important to note that even the discourse of Adu Boahen had shifted from 'stolen verdict to 'bought verdict'.

According to Gyimah-Boadi (1994:85), the 1992 return to a liberal democratic constitution was a step towards democracy despite its numerous flaws. Political liberalisation, constitutionalism, the rule of law, judicial independence, press freedom etc. were all put on the political agenda. By 1996, the conditions under which elections were held had improved significantly. According to Ernest Dumor, a member of Ghana's Electoral Commission,

> The 1996 Election indicates that by paying attention to the techno-structure, the structural and functional arrangements of government apparatus and process which allow for an effective participation and competition through multiparty system, the foundation is being laid for a stable society (Dumor 1998).

> He adds that the participation of numerous nonpartisan civil society organisations in election monitoring and civic education helped greatly in ensuring free and fair elections.

In the Ghanaian model, the charismatic redeemer might tamper with electoral mechanisms to ensure that his victory is not in jeopardy. However, as soon as his legitimacy has stabilised, transparent electoral rules might be allowed.

The Problematic of Democratic Transition

There has been an intense and passionate debate over Ghana's political future with different, sometimes contradictory, views expressed on whether democracy in the country is advancing or regressing (Ninsin 1996). It seems clear, however, that liberalism is advancing and the political system is stabilising. The attitudinal survey carried out by the Centre for Democracy and Development reveals that democracy is the preferred form of government for 76.5 percent of the Ghanaian population (CDD 1999:15). The report also suggests that democratic values seem to be widely accepted in the country.

The question being posed now on democratic transition in Ghana is whether the country's democracy is deepening. One way of approaching the question is to examine the much acclaimed decentralisation process, which is supposed to have taken democracy to the grassroots. In 1998, Ghana celebrated the first decade of its decentralisation programme, which was set in motion in 1988. This shift towards a more decentralised administration has been massively supported by donor agencies as an example to the rest of the African continent. The agencies supporting it include The World Bank's capacity-building initiative, the United Nations Development Programme (UNDP) capacity development and utilisation programme, United States Agency for International Development (USAID) democracy and governance programme, the European Union, the Netherlands Development Organisation (SNW), the German Cooperation Agency (GTZ), the British Department for International Development (DFID), the Canadian International Development Agency (CIDA), and the Danish International Development Agency (DANIDA),

Decentralisation in Ghana is an interesting case study because there has been a history of strong resistance to regionalisation and decentralisation of power in Ghana since 1950. President Kwame Nkrumah considered regionalisation and decentralisation as opening the door to the destabilisation of national unity and cohesion. From 1950 when he took over the administration of the country to his overthrow in 1966, Nkrumah dismantled the regional structure bequeathed by the British and pursued a policy of centralised administration, which in fact continued till 1988. It is therefore interesting to find out what has changed after ten years of the new policy of decentralisation.

In 1988 the number of districts in the country was increased from 65 to 110 and they were regrouped into ten regions. The step was in part a result of pressure from the IMF that Ghana should democratise its polity and introduce good governance. The key concepts that the international financial agencies insisted upon were popular participation, accountability and efficiency. The objective of decentralisation was defined as empowerment of the people. Elections were held for the district assemblies in 1988 and 1994 and the next elections were scheduled for May 1998. The elections were however organised on a nonpartisan basis and political parties were not allowed to present candidates. People contested as individuals and the state paid for the electoral campaign. The idea was to create opportunities for high quality and known local candidates who might not have the financial resources or party support to contest effectively in a party competitive framework.

The District Assemblies were given an unprecedented number of functions, including deliberative, legislative and executive ones. Eighty-six specific functions aimed at promoting development, including natural resource development, primary and secondary education and infrastructure development were allocated to the District Assemblies. They were to operate twenty-two functional departments to carry them out.

It seems fair to say that there have been real achievements through this programme. There has been the development of considerable local initiative and self-help spirit in local governance. A significant improvement in the provision of basic amenities and infrastructure has taken place — constitutionally, five percent of public expenditure is allocated to the districts. A new crop of national politicians with a local base who had been groomed in the districts has emerged — about 30 percent of the current Parliament are drawn from this new breed of politicians.

But there are shortcomings too. Too many functions have been allocated to the districts and available funds are not sufficient to enable the latter to perform effectively. Increasingly, NGOs, especially religious ones, are now stepping in to provide services and the district authorities are losing their legitimacy. District personnel are poorly trained. Most civil servants are not prepared to leave Accra to go and work in the districts. Professional staff of the districts — engineers, doctors, teachers — are still recruited and are under the control of the central bureaucracy in Accra.

The democratic credentials of the decentralisation policy are reduced by the fact that the district chief executive is not elected but instead is appointed by the President and approved by the district assembly. A third of the district assembly is also nominated by the President, and they are usually 'big men' who overshadow the locally elected members.

Perhaps the most striking conclusion of most of the Ghanaian scholars with whom I have discussed this issue is that the real objective of the decentralisation programme has been to provide a rural political base for President Jerry Rawlings. This has served him well by enabling him to win elections and stabilise the political system. But the objective of empowering the people has so far been set aside.

At a more general level, the real test of democratic transition in Ghana came in the year 2000. Rawlings was not qualified to run. Nor did he attempt to change the Constitution to enable him to do so. It seems fair to say that the successful organisation of the 2000 elections enhanced and deepened Ghana's democracy. Indeed, as Kwesi Jonah (1998) argued before the time, democratic consolidation is occurring in spite of the bleak economic situation, because opposition parties have come to accept electoral politics as the only way to a more prosperous and stable future. In addition, grassroots interest in the use of the vote to effect political change has increased considerably (Abdul-Wahabi 1998).

The Ghanaian model of democratic transition that we have outlined demonstrates a high level of political voluntarism organised by a certain Jerry Rawlings. It involves the seizure of power by the force of arms and its maintenance for about a decade by a high level of repression and an effective security apparatus. The next stage is pacification and the reconstruction of state institutions as well as the establishment of state authority in the hinterland through local government reforms. There is then the organisation of relatively free and fair elections and, as it transpired, the arrival of political alternation in the new millennium. It is essentially a model about the reconstruction of the state as a prelude to democratic transformation. It is a model and thus a pointer on what needs to be done by other countries in the region and we believe the neighbours have been watching.

3

Nigeria

Introduction

The story of Nigeria is very traumatic as far as democratic transition is concerned. Historically, Nigeria was one of the few countries in Africa that had a significant reputation for protecting human rights and civil liberties. In fact, one could talk of a certain democratic tradition in the country's political culture. A long succession of military regimes that have conducted Nigerian affairs during most of its post-independence life, however, have eroded this tradition. Initially, the military regimes were constrained to bottle up their authoritarian habits and conduct the nation's affairs in a fairly civil manner. The first act of a military regime after a coup d'état is to suspend the Constitution. However, only the sections of the Constitution that regulate partisan politics are usually suspended while the other sections, especially those that define the functions and powers of the judiciary and the human rights clause are left to function. Things gradually change and the military stop pretending to have any respect for the nation's laws. Be that as it may, there is a rich but contradictory democratic tradition embedded in Nigerian civil society although the pattern of primitive capital accumulation in the country and the impact of military rule had devastating consequences on this democratic tradition.

Militarism and State Character

The mlitary has ruled Nigeria for 29 out of the 43 years in which the country has existed as an independent entity. The armed forces have made grievous inroads into the country's culture and institutions. Their influence has been extremely negative on society through the spread of their authoritarian values, which are in essence anti-social and destructive of politics. By 'politics' we imply the art of negotiating conflicts related to the exercise of power. However, in Nigeria, the pace and nature of the so-called programme of transition to democratic rule have been dictated by military fiat. There is a decline in civility and a rise in violence in social interaction. In terms of governance, the most devastating impact of the military has been to spread the myth that they have a useful political role as an institution that could use its 'monopoly' of force to prevent chaos. It will be recalled that since the Gowon era, the military regimes have used the 'impending chaos' argument to postpone promised democratisation.

The long period of military rule has destroyed Nigerian federalism, sacrificing it on the altar of over-centralisation. The military are structurally unsuited to the running of a federal system because their unified command structure is incapable of accepting that a state government, which they consider to be hierarchically subordinate to the federal government, could have domains over which she is sovereign. Nigeria's geopolitical realities have been completely modified. The tripartite structure which had become quadripartite with the creation of the Mid-West in 1963, has changed drastically as a result of the multiplication of states whose number, now, stands at 36. This proliferation of states has produced a Jacobin effect that strengthens the centre by eroding the autonomy of the regions. Nigeria thus finds itself now with a so-called Federation that is for all practical purposes a unitary state, with only a limited devolution of power to the states. Enormous powers, hitherto held by the regions or the cabinet, have been allocated to the President or the Governor in the 1979 and 1999 Constitutions. With the reversal of Nigeria's federal tradition, the guarantee that was used to help reduce the fears of ethno-regional domination was lost.

Under the Sani Abacha regime, Nigeria moved fully into the terrain of tyranny and the impact of militarism on the character of the state was extensively expressed. Numerous parallel security agencies were established to terrorise Nigerians into accepting Abacha's self-succession plans. They include the Office of the National Security Adviser under Ismaila Gwarzo, a retired police officer, and the Office of the Chief Security Officer to the Head of State under Major Hamza Al Mustapha. Mustapha controlled a Special Strike Force that was not integrated into the army. In addition there were the Directorate of Military Intelligence under General Ibrahim Sabo, the Defence Intelligence Agency, and the Brigade of Guards. These were in addition to the formally constituted security agencies — mainly, the State Security Service and the National Intelligence Agency. At the state level, military governors established their own 'terrorist units' — Lagos State (Operation Sweep), Ogun State (Operation Wedge), Oyo State (Operation Gbole), Imo State (Operation Storm), Rivers State (Operation Wipe-out), Adamawa State (Operation Zaki), and Bauchi State (Operation Kwanta Kwanta). These were operations directed at terrorising the population and carrying out very high levels of extrajudicial killings (CDHR 1997:5). The security outfits were given the 'license to kill', which they apparently used liberally, especially with the assassinations of notable opposition figures.

To create favourable conditions for Abacha's self-succession plans, all those who had explicit political ambitions or were openly critical of the regime were accused of various crimes and detained or jailed. M.K.O. Abiola was detained for four years, until his death in July 1998. Also detained was the former and current Head of State and internationally respected elder statesman, General Olusegun Obasanjo; his former deputy, Shehu Yar Adua, who had presidential ambitions and who died in detention under suspicious circumstances; and numerous others. In all, over thirty people were accused of plotting a coup in March 1995 and sentenced to long jail terms. In March 1997, treason charges were filed against leading opposition leaders in exile. They included Professor Wole Soyinka, Nigeria's Nobel Laureate, Chief Anthony Enaharo and General Alani Akinrinade of NADECO. On 21 December 1997, the regime announced the arrest of its second in command, General Diya and many other senior officers who were tried for treason and were about to be executed when Abacha suddenly died. Many politicians such as Bola Ige and Abubakar Rimi, Second Republic Governors of Oyo and Kano States, Senator Lam Adesina, Comrade Ola Oni, Alhaji Sule Lamido, Olu Falae and others were also detained or imprisoned. Human rights activists such as Olisa Agbakoba, convener of United Action for Democracy, Beko Ransome Kuti, and Segun Maiyegun of the Campaign for Democracy, and Femi Falana of the CDHR suffered the same fate. Numerous trade unionists, journalists, religious leaders, army officers, even Nigerian ambassadors abroad were all detained for disloyalty to Abacha.

The level of extrajudicial killings was very high. Many notable members of the opposition, whom the regime felt were a threat, were assassinated by armed gangs suspected to be state agents. These include Alfred Rewane, killed in his house by armed men. He was alleged to have been one of the financiers of NADECO, the opposition coalition. Kudirat Abiola, the vocal wife of the detained winner of the June 1993 elections, M. K. O. Abiola, was also slain by armed agents in 1996. Bagauda Kalto, the Kaduna correspondent of *The News* magazine, was bombed. The explanation was that the regime was embarrassed that a 'Northerner' was writing revealing articles for a magazine that the regime was presenting as a 'Southwestern mouth-piece'. On 8 December 1997, General Shehu Yar'Adua, an ardent opponent of Abacha's self-succession plan, fell into a coma in prison and died in suspicious circumstances.

Agents of the regime behaved as thugs and rogues. Col. Peter Ogar, Military Administrator of Kwara State, for example, interrupted a church service he was attending for the celebration of Nigeria's 37th Independence Anniversary in Ilorin, took over the pulpit, and poured venom on Catholic Bishops for daring to warn Abacha against the temptation of self-succession (*Post Express* 10/3/1997). Government security agents abducted Moshood Fayemiwo, editor of *Razor* magazine, from a United Nations refugee camp in Benin Republic. The Foreign Minister, Tom Ikimi described President Nelson Mandela as an irresponsible man who could not keep his wife, and regularly called ambassadors to his Ministry and insulted them. Nigeria had been turned into a terrorist state.

Corruption

It was not the military that introduced corruption into Nigeria's body politic. From the mid-1950s onwards, all the Regional governments were involved in major corruption scandals. In 1957, the Forster Sutton Commission found that Nnamdi Azikiwe had placed public funds in his private bank, the African Continental Bank. In 1963, it was the turn of the Coker Commission to reveal that, in the Western Region, Awolowo had appropriated public resources for his own personal use. Other examples are not lacking. Indeed, it would appear that in all the Regions, political entrepreneurs took over the control of political parties, a strategy which enabled them to embark on primitive accumulation of capital (Ibrahim 1991). During the successive military and civilian regimes, the extraction of public resources for personal use increased significantly. The relatively large size and scope of the Nigerian economy, coupled with the manna from petroleum, contributed to this state of affairs.

Although it did not initiate it, the Nigerian military entrenched the culture of public corruption established by earlier civilian regimes. It was a major change in the country's political culture; in the past, corruption was corruption — unethical or illegal advantages procured through official positions. Gradually, the military became power drunk and started believing they could banalise corruption and use their monopoly of force to prevent Nigerians complaining about it. The turning point in this regard was General Gowon's attempt to prevent the swearing of affidavits containing accusations of corruption against leading members of his regime. Since then, a lot of water has passed under the bridge. Under administrations of Generals Babangida, Abacha and Abubakar, what used to be known as corruption became the art of government itself. There was a complete prebendalisation of state power and virtually all acts by public officials involving public expenditure or public goods of any kind would lead to the appropriation of state finances or property by officials. The routine operations of government were subjected to prebendal rules. For example, state governments and parastatals had to pay, as they put it, 'up front' a percentage of their statutory allocations to the Presidency, Ministry of Finance and Central Bank officials before their allocations were released. They in turn, simply took their own personal shares, 'up front', from government coffers. Contractors who used to bribe officials for government contracts were completely sidelined. The President, military governors, ministers and so on simply allocated contracts to their own front companies, and they did not even have to pretend that they were doing the job because nobody could dare pose such questions. The country's major resource, petroleum, was being allocated to individuals who would then sell them to the petroleum companies. The military succeeded in transforming corruption from a deviant activity by public officials into the *raison d'être* of the Nigerian state.

The security machine was also used to take the theft of state resources to an all-high level. Abacha's chief security operative, Ismaila Gwarzo, was said to have withdrawn over 10 million dollars as part of the security vote. Dr Paul Ogwuna, the Governor of the Central Bank explained that Abacha signed personally for the monies in his capacity as the chief accounting officer.[5] 'The signature of the head of state is law. Refusal to honour it is regarded as sabotage. The Central Bank of Nigeria was therefore obeying "lawful authority"' (*Vanguard* 17/8/1998).

On 9 November 1998, the Press Officer to the Abubakar Administration, Mohammed Haruna, announced to the country that in the days following the sudden death of Sani Abacha, vast sums of money had been discovered in various caches belonging to the late tyrant. The amonts of cash already discovered — $625.263 million, £75.306 million and 252 million Naira — totalled in all 66.4 billion Naira (*Punch* 11/12/98). The amount represented 25 percent of the 1998 budget of the country, which was 260 billion Naira. Reports filtering in from the ongoing investigations indicated that the monies so far recovered were a small part of the national resources looted by Abacha and his henchmen. The implication is that a significant part of the country's revenue was simply being pocketed by a few individuals. The former finance minister, Anthony Ani has for example announced that the former National Security Adviser, Ismaila Gwarzo had withdrawn $917 million before December 1997, and $419 million between January and May 1998 for security operations. The cheques for these amounts were directly authorised by the Head of State and they did not go through the Ministry of Finance.

According to Atiku Abubakar, the current Vice President, $2.2 billion suspected to be stolen loot, has been traced to Abacha's Swiss accounts (*ThisDay*, 20/10/99). In his budget presentation address to the National Assembly, President Obasanjo revealed that government estimates indicated that about $20 billion had been illegally looted from Nigeria and banked abroad out of which $119,768,530 had been recovered since he assumed office. In addition, $600 million in private accounts were frozen while attempts to recover them continued (*New Nigerian* 25/11/99). The scale of corruption in Nigeria had become completely outrageous.

Civil Society

Nigeria has had a vibrant civil society in which the mass media, trades and professional unions, students' associations, community organisations and human and civil rights groups have been able to act as an effective counter-weight against the state. The Nigerian media, in particular, has been able to maintain substantial freedom in spite of draconian attempts by the state to control it. With independence, colonial anti-press laws were strengthened instead of being liberalised. In 1962 an Official Secrets Act was enacted (It was under this law that *Newbreed* and *Newswatch* magazines were proscribed in 1978 and 1987 respectively). Using these laws and often going beyond them, government imprisoned, detained, tortured, harassed and often sacked numerous journalists for writing things that were unpalatable to the state. Much more disturbing was the murder of Dele Giwa, a popular journalist, by a parcel bomb in 1986. This is the first case of murder in the 140-year-old history of Nigerian journalism. During the Abacha regime (1993–1998), a new phase unfolded in which critical journalists were systematically harassed, detained at will, sometimes falsely charged and convicted for treason and coup plotting, and a number were assassinated. In spite of this reign of terror, a section of the press remained bold and vigorous in its criticism of rising authoritarianism (Ya'u 1997).

The dynamism of trades, professional and students' unions in Nigeria is one of the clearest signs of the democratic drive embedded in its civil society. For example, Nigerian students have played a very significant role since 1934 when they established the Lagos Youth Movement, the core on which the first nationalist party, the NCNC was built. In the post war years, the West African Students' Union played a galvanising role in the independence movements. The spontaneous students' demonstrations that followed the assassination of the popular General Murtala Mohammed in February 1976 helped in preventing the retrogressive Dimka-led coup d'état. As the study by Shettima (1997) shows, Nigerian students have continued to play a significant role in the country's democratic struggles.

In the case of the Academic Staff Union of Universities (ASUU), radicalisation was a product of the trade union struggles in which lecturers found themselves involved in order to improve their conditions of work, enhance academic freedom and enhance the quality of university education. Other professional associations such as the Nigerian Bar Association (NBA) and even the National Association of Resident Doctors and the Nigerian Medical Association have struggled for improved social services. Since the NLC's Workers' Charter of Demands in 1980 and National Association of Nigerian Students (NANS) Charter of Demands in 1982, there has been a growing consciousness that specific economic and social demands could be met only if the frontiers of democracy were broadened. A. O. Olukoshi (1997) draws attention to the significant role which the Left has played in promoting the social and economic demands of the people. He argues also that the Left itself has been transformed over time and become much more committed to the promotion of liberal democratic rights. From the point of view of the state, however, there was a growing 'counter-consciousness' that the Nigerian bourgeoisie could only be protected by restricting human rights and tightening the frontiers of democracy. This accounts for the frequent ban orders, the termination of appointments, detentions and other repressive measures to which unions, professional organisations and their leaders were subjected. Increased repression was further reinforced by the difficulties faced by the Nigerian state in its attempt to impose the IMF-inspired structural adjustment programme, which was strongly resisted by Nigerian civil society (Olukoshi 1993).

Nigeria also has a large community of lawyers, which developed right from the colonial period. For these lawyers, most of whom are in private practice, to be able to maintain their elevated place in society, the judicial machine must operate are in a fairly just and non arbitrary manner. In other words, the average plaintiffs should be convinced that the lawyer could make a difference in solving their problem and are thus ready to pay the necessary fees. Lawyers therefore had a corporate interest in the maintenance of due process, the rule of law and civil liberties. The fact that lawyers became a powerful pressure group as well as the technocrats that drafted Nigerian Constitutions and laws played an important role in maintaining this legal culture. In addition, they were able to guide subsequent military regimes to keep to the form even if not to the spirit of judicial process. Military regimes, for example, were constrained to enact new decrees that would repeal or bypass existing laws that hindered their objectives, rather than act in a 'might is right' manner. This legal fetishism often transgressed the course of justice and the spirit of the law but to a certain extent, legalism slows down political arbitrariness especially as, until recently, no law or decree in Nigeria has been retroactive.

The principles of the rule of law however have been increasingly threatened by the state in recent years. Decree no. 2 of 1984 allowed the Chief of General Staff to detain citizens for extended periods without charging them in court. The decree suspended the important instrument of *Habeas Corpus* that citizens could use to compel the state to produce detainees in court. The Nigerian legal system has continued in a fairly combative mood. In 1984, the whole legal profession rose against the suspension of due process and systematisation of military tribunals to 'persecute' rather than 'prosecute' politicians. They tried, even if with limited success, to resist the authoritarian excesses of the Babangida regime. The assassination of Dele Giwa, editor of *Newswatch* magazine, for example, led to an important civil liberties case. Dele Giwa was said to have been interrogated and threatened just before his death by Colonel Halilu Akilu, the Director of Military Security and Lt. Col. A. K. Togun, Deputy Director of State Security, over a lead story he was preparing. In spite of the suspicious circumstances that surrounded his death, the Director of Public Prosecutions was unwilling to prosecute the two officers. It was left to a private lawyer, Gani Fawehinmi, to take the matter up in court. In a historic judgement delivered on 18 December 1987, the Supreme Court authorised private persons to prosecute criminal cases that were not pursued by the Public Prosecution Department.

In recent years, the struggle by lawyers and other activists for human rights has been assuming a sharper organisational focus. In the first place, the Nigerian Bar Association (NBA) became more openly assertive of its commitment to the rule of law and democratisation until it was destroyed following protracted struggles by Government agents to take over its leadership in 1993. In 1985, an Association of Democratic Lawyers of Nigeria (ADLN) and in 1989 a 'Committee for the Defence of Human Rights' (CDHR) under the chairmanship of a medical doctor and human rights crusader, Dr Beko Ransome-Kuti, were formed. One of the most significant developments in this regard was the formation in October 1987 of the Civil Liberties Organisation (CLO) which emerged to co-ordinate the struggle for civil liberties. In December 1988, the CLO published a report on Human Rights Violation in Nigeria as a working document to help in the fight against arbitrariness by the state and its agents. It became the norm that many other similar organisations were to follow. Other notable human rights organisations were the Constitutional Rights Project and the Committee for the Defence of Human Rights.

This brief overview of the Nigerian mass media, trades and professional unions, the legal system and human rights organisations reveals clearly that the history of democratic struggles in Nigeria has not been limited to the formal political process. Nigerians have been forced to expand the terrain on which they struggle for the expansion of democratic space (Ibrahim 1997). It is clear that there are a number of democratic assets embedded in the country's civil society and their force and relevance lies in the relative autonomy they have enjoyed vis-à-vis the state. This autonomy is frequently subjected to serious threats by the state but the capacity for resistance has been significantly high. Yet, the preservation of democracy is not a simple function of assets and problems, it is also a question of historical will. Nigerians have demonstrated a will to preserve hard won democratic rights, and if they are trained in the art of provocation, they are also trained in the art of compromise.

Gender Politics of the State: From the First Lady to the First Daughter

Given the long period of military rule and the male-centred nature of the armed forces, it is not surprising that women have played a marginal role in Nigeria's public life. The public profile of elite women only changed dramatically with the coming into power of First Lady Chief-Dr-Mrs Maryam Babangida, wife of General Babangida. Mrs Babangida had first assumed prominence in 1983 when her husband became Chief of Army Staff. On that basis, she became the president of the Nigerian Army Officers' Wives Association. It was at that point that she started seeing herself as a leader (Mama 1997:88). When her husband became president, she opened a First Lady office for herself in the presidency and became a prominent figure in Nigeria's public life. This was the first time that the wife of a Nigerian Head of State would use her spousal position to launch a career in public life.

In 1987, five years after Mrs Rawlings had established her organisation, Mrs Babangida launched the Better Life for Rural Women Programme (BLP). The wives of all senior state officials were incorporated into the organisation. The wives of military governors in the states became chairpersons of the state BLP and wives of local government chairpersons acted likewise at their level. Considerable state resources were channelled either officially or unofficially to the BLP. At least 400 million Naira was officially allocated to the BLP in its first five years. The BLP claimed to have made a major contribution to improving the lot of rural women. The claims include the organisation of 10,000 co-operatives, 1,793 cottage industries, 2,397 farms, 470 women's centres and 233 health centres (Mama 1997:92). Most serious observers however, were of the view that these figures were concocted, and that nothing tangible, except the boosting of Mariam Babangida's image, had been achieved. As Phil Okeke (1998:18) has argued, the BLP was simply a forum for the display of power, influence and prestige by privileged women, leaving behind the disadvantaged rural women. Indeed, Maryam Babangida's style of running the BLP was very authoritarian and indeed militaristic. She issued orders from the state house and expected them to be obeyed without discussion. She always stressed that she was not interested in feminism or women's liberation but in promoting wifehood and motherhood (Mama 1997:93).

In 1990, the National Commission for Women (NCW) was established as the official state organ charged with handling women's issues. The establishment of the NCW was in fact first announced in President Babangida's message to the launching of Maryam's biography, *The Home Front* on 19 September 1988. Maryam Babangida therefore must have believed it was created for her. When however the NCW under the leadership of Professor Bolanle Awe tried to establish the organisation as an autonomous body with full competence in handling all issues relating to women, Maryam became very upset. It was as if her offspring was trying to become a rival organisation. She therefore continuously harassed the chair, Professor Bolanle Awe, and even had her detained by security officials. Eventually, Mrs Babangida made her husband reconstitute the Board of the NCW and place it under the office of the First Lady.

To establish a permanent place for herself in history, Mrs Babangida obtained public money through her husband which she used to establish a huge edifice in Abuja valued at 1.6 billion Naira ($16 million). This edifice was christened the Maryam Babangida Centre for Women and Development. In 1992 when it appeared that they might have to leave office soon, Mrs Babangida applied to the Corporate Affairs Commission to register the Centre as a Trust, with her and her son Mohammed as Trustees for life. The application was queried by the Commission because they had not gone through due process in advertising the Trust in three national dailies, and obtaining a security clearance (*The News* 25/7/94). The Centre was registered as she had wished anyway as a property of MIB (Maryam Ibrahim Babangida) Foundation.

Maryam Babangida was imperial in her conduct and often behaved as if she was the co-president of the country. According to Professor Bolaji Akinyemi, former foreign minister, she summoned him in the name of her husband one night to dress him down. She had tried to organise a cocktail reception for ECOWAS Ambassadors and their wives and when she noticed that the minister was not keen, she had gone ahead and organised it with the protocol division anyway. She chose a date in August 1987 and realised on that same evening that most of the ambassadors were out of the country, on annual leave, and would be represented by rather junior officers. She cancelled the event that night, summoned and informed the minister in the presence of her husband that she had 'a joint-right with the President to appoint a new Minister of External Affairs' (*The News* 25/10/93). Shortly thereafter, Bolaji Akinyemi was sacked and a new minister appointed. That event, argued Akinyemi, signalled the beginning of a Joint Imperial Presidency.

In that 'joint imperial presidency', Maryam was often assumed to be the worst villain. Wole Soyinka indeed once argued that rather than worry about Ibrahim Babangida's hidden agenda, one should worry more about Maryam Babangida's, given that 'First Ladyism and its attendant sycophancy had burgeoned into outrageous proportions' (*Tempo* 17/11/94). She was often considered responsible for making her husband personalise and prebendalise government business. There were even insinuations that she was the real power behind the throne. It was widely assumed for example that major state appointments depended more on the whims and caprices of the First Lady than on the wishes of their husbands, the substantive Heads of State.

In 1993, General Sani Abacha took over power and his wife, Mariam Abacha, became the First Lady and occupied the office established by her predecessor. Her eldest daughter, Zainab, then had the brilliant idea of opening her own office as the First Daughter in the Presidency.

Mariam Abacha was a very interventionist First Lady. She was, for example, very involved in obtaining state jobs or contracts for her friends and cronies. She herself recently explained in a BBC interview that although she was not taking decisions herself, Ministers and even foreign diplomats who were seeking an appointment with her husband should come and see her first to arrange it (*Punch* 4/11/99). In their 'professional careers' as wives of army officers, Mariam Abacha had developed a bitter rivalry with Maryam Babangida. Having got her turn, she set out to dismantle her predecessor's work. The BLP was dissolved and a 'new' one, the Family Support Programme (FSP), was established. A state instrument to implement it, the Family Economic Advancement Programme, was set in motion and significant state funds were devoted to it. State officials were incorporated into the structure just as Maryam Babangida had arranged. The Maryam Babangida Centre for Women and Development was taken over by the state, in spite of the registration as a private trust, thus depriving Maryam the ownership of the structure that was to have guaranteed her a place in history.

These two femocrats generated a lot of negative reactions and publicity for women in general and for the gender equality struggle in particular. They were patriarchal, showy and arrogant, in a society which expected women to be self-effacing, shy and modest. Many men, and indeed women, would never forgive them for that. Their arrogance and disdain for the lot of

ordinary women were seized upon by sexists, as evidence of the futility of struggling against gender discrimination. They were also women who became fabulously rich on the basis of extracting state resources without any accountability. Maryam Babangida for example was said to be worth at least $2 billion (*The News* 4/10/93). They used their positions to coerce ministers, state governors, heads of parastatals and businessmen to donate huge sums of mostly public money to them, to please their husbands. At a more dramatic level, it brought the question of the use of female sexuality to enhance female power, known in Nigeria as 'bottom power', into the centre of the political debate. Bottom power as one writer has described it is any avenue available to women for exerting their sexuality in order to gain favour from men both as individuals and as authorities with access to social opportunities and privileges. Bottom power attracts very strong social disaffection from men and women alike (Okeke 1998:17).

The basic thesis of bottom power is extremely sexist as it assumes that female achievers have obtained their positions or their wealth through the exploitation of their sexuality rather than through their other skills. It has buttressed beer parlour male chauvinism, where the feeling is expressed that women use what they have to get what they need, so they don't deserve any special consideration. The prominence of bottom power theme under femocracy has been used to oppose demands for affirmative action in favour of women. As Amina Mama concluded on the question of femocracy in Nigeria:

> Femocracy has affected the gender politics of the nation, but not in the way that one might have hoped. It cannot be said to have enhanced gender equality or to have in any way challenged conservative attitudes to women. Instead, eight years of femocracy has generated promises to appoint token women, and has made the parading of expensively attired wives into a political tradition (Mama 1997:97).

Indeed, it has been pointed out for example that Maryam Babangida ensured that no woman became a minister during her husband's eight-year rule and that she personally was responsible that the only female director-general, Mrs Franscesca Emmanuel, was sacked from her job (*The News* 4/10/93). Presumably Mrs Babangida wanted to be the only female light that was shining.

The current elected President, General Olusegun Obasanjo has publicly declared that he has no First Lady, he only has a wife[6]. His wife therefore does not (yet) have an official office in the Presidency. She did not play an overt political role in government policy-making and implementation in the early months of her husband's Presidency. Be that as it may, the concept of the First Lady has become entrenched. Stella Obasanjo has already convened a meeting of wives of state governors. She has presided over many occasions in which the issue of women and children have been discussed. Her husband has had to stop her from taking a huge official delegation on a trip to the Caribbean. In November 1999, she advertised in the newspapers that she was setting up two new organisations, the Stella Obasanjo Foundation, the trustees for which are Chief Stella Obasanjo, Dr John Abebe and Professor Olikoye Ransome-Kuti (*Punch* 4/11/99), and the Child Care Trust with the trustees Chief Stella Obasanjo, Dr John Abebe, Professor Olikoye Ransome-Kuti and Professor Ibrahim Gambari (*Vanguard* 4/11/99).[7] The Child Care Trust, to tackle problems of poverty, unemployment, nutrition, health and education as they affect children, was to be launched in January 2000 (*Punch* 24/11/99). In January 2000, President Obasanjo directed that the office of the First Lady be abolished. By the end of Obasanjo's first year in office, Stella Obasanjo had opened the office of the First Lady — that was bigger than her two predecessors'. We believe that it is possible and desirable for presidents and presidential spouses to make positive contributions towards enhancing gender equality in their society, but only if they guard against the pitfalls of femocracy.

Elections Without Choice

Elections have meaning for most people only in a democratic context because they lead to the choice of decision-makers by the majority. But Nigeria has a long history of electoral rigging and fraud. In addition, constitutional provisions hamper the free workings of a fair multiparty system. For example, Sections 201 and 202 of the 1979 Constitution and 221 and 222 of the 1999 Constitution specifically *limit* the definition of a political party to an organisation *recognised by the state* to canvass for votes. The law forbids any organisation not so recognised to seek voters' support. More importantly, both on the juridical and political levels, parties could no longer be considered as popular organisations that aggregate and articulate interests and opinions but as corporate entities that are registered with the state. This has meant that the political significance of parties was no longer determined by popular support, as is the case in all democratic countries in the world, but by administrative fiat.[8] Another serious impediment to free choice was that party nominees had to have security clearance from the state to be recognised as genuine nominees. It was not enough for candidates to secure their nomination, the soldiers in charge of state security had to declare that the candidate was suitable before he or she would be allowed to contest any election under the various transitions to democratic rule.

The most serious limitation on free choice during the long transition to democratic rule was the annulment of the June 12, 1993 presidential election.

In a last ditch attempt to get General Babangida to hand over power, the two parties, the Social Democratic Party (SDP) and National Republican Convention (NRC) had virtually nominated close personal friends and business associates of President Babangida as their presidential candidates. They were M. K. O. Abiola for the SDP and Bashir Tofa for the NRC. After much procrastination by government and determined protest against another postponement by the people, presidential elections were finally held on June 12, 1993. The candidate of the SDP won neatly in an election that was surprisingly considered in general free and fair. The elections were in our view a sort of referendum in which Nigerians voted Babangida out, and made clear that they wished the military to step down. The General however refused to take no for an answer. He cancelled the elections and tried to initiate yet another round of 'political crafting'. Thereupon ensued massive protests. Babangida had to leave power in haste and handover to an incompetent and powerless civilian without any mandate, creating the basis for yet another coup d'état in November 1993 by his former second in command, General Abacha. The question of the annulled mandate however was to haunt all subsequent Nigerian politics.

The Problematic of Democratic Transition

The politically acute Nigerian press discerned after two to three years of the regime that General Babangida had a hidden agenda, which involved using the so-called programme of transition to civilian rule as a ploy to cling to power for as long as possible. While launching the Political Bureau in January 1986, General Babangida had announced that power would be handed over to a democratically elected civilian regime in 1990. The Report of the Political Bureau confirmed this date. He however stuck to power till August 1993, when he was finally pushed out of power by his equally ambitious military colleagues. At every twist and turn of the convoluted transition programme, the Babangida's government tried to create conditions that would bring about the collapse of the process.

An interminable democratic transition programme, therefore, was turned into an instrument in the hands of the ruling elite reluctant to lose its power and privileges. In 1985, General Babangida carried out a palace coup d'état against the Buhari regime under which he was serving. He was able to carry forward the military project of destabilising the political class and imposing a militaristic conception of politics on the country. In addition, he pushed forward the transformation of the military into a virtual ruling class:

> The military regime have capitalised on the structural adjustment program to strengthen its control over the political process, contained

and domesticated the civilian faction of the bourgeoisie, imposed its 'hegemony' over the pattern of political and economic reproduction and actually laid the foundation for the continuation of military rule beyond the on-going transition program (Ihonvbere 1991:23).

The military faction of the bourgeoisie was henceforth leading not only in wealth, but also in the control of the politico-administrative apparatus of the state.

The military closely supervised the design and implementation of the transition programme to ensure that it was in conformity with their world-view. They used university intellectuals to produce the drafts and brought in military officers to fine-tune the programme (Ibrahim 1997). The first concern of the soldiers and their intellectual friends was to destabilise the country's political class. The military was conscious that previous military attempts to control the political process had been derailed by politicians. In 1986, the military junta announced a ten-year ban on certain well-known politicians. In September 1987, the ban was extended to the totality of those who had held political office in all proceeding civilian and military regimes and in 1989, to all those who had been heads of the various transition agencies. A new breed of 'grassroot politicians', 'untainted' by multiparty politics was to be created. The idea was that grassroots persons elected in the 1987 non-party local government elections were suitable material for the formation of the new breed parties.

The Babangida regime rejected a multiparty framework and proposed a two party system with both parties requiring state registration. To determine the two political parties to be registered, the National Electoral Commission (NEC) and the government imposed very expensive and virtually impossible preconditions that only the upper section of the bourgeoisie or old politicians with established networks could have afforded or met. In three months, the parties were to establish well-equipped offices with at least three paid staff in all the 435 local government areas in the country. In addition, they were to supply 25 membership lists of their parties comprising the names, photographs and personal details of at least 200 members from each local government in the country (making at least 87,000 individual membership files per party) to the NEC. For good measure, prospective parties were to submit their applications with a registration fee of 50,000 Naira. In spite of these draconian measures, 13 parties were able to submit their files before the deadline[9]. In a broadcast to the nation on 6 October 1989, the Head of State in a perfect Catch-22 scenario used the argument that the 'impossible' preconditions had not been perfectly adhered to as a justification to refuse to register any of the parties. I believe that it was at this point that Babangida made his strategic blunder. If he had followed the Rawlings model at that point when he still had credibility, established his own party, and used the state machine and the considerable fortune he had accumulated, he could have succeeded in getting himself elected as Nigeria's president.

Rather than do that, he concentrated on what he called political craftsmanship. He tried to develop a specific type of political party based on the idea that a mass party should know all its members and have files on them — a very military conception. To control the political process, the military under Babangida were ready to deny the reality of democratic parties, such as differential levels of commitment and the existence of party militants who would want to register, and sympathisers who might not bother to register but might vote for the party. In addition, the whole idea of democratic elections is that attempts are made by candidates to persuade voters to transfer their loyalty from one party to another, so adherence to parties is never a rigid bureaucratic issue. Their insistence that the politicians of the Third Republic must have no contacts or connections with politicians of the former regimes was clearly mischievous. Similarly, the rule that wealthy people must not play a major role in the parties or use their money to win votes, at a time when their economic policies were creating a tiny minority of excessively wealthy people in a sea of mass poverty was nothing short of pure mischief.

The government eventually decided to dissolve all the thirteen parties. One of the closest political advisers of the military admitted that the parties were dissolved because none of them met the vision and objectives of the military administration (Olagunju et al. 1993:214). The military wanted 100 percent control of the parties. The next step they took was to create two new parties, allegedly for the 'ordinary people' — the Social Democratic Party and the National Republican Convention, with the former leaning 'a little to the left of centre' and the latter leaning 'a little to the right of the centre'. It was under this military direction that government drew up the manifestos and constitutions of the two parties, and decided to fund and staff them, before calling on individuals (as opposed to organised groups) to sign up.

Apart from imposing manifestos and constitutions on the two parties, excessive powers were given to government-appointed Administrative Secretaries to organise their establishment and to exclude radicals, socialists, anti-Structural Adjustment Programme agitators as well as alleged ideological and religious extremists. In addition, Decree 48 of 1991 gave the National Electoral Commission (NEC), established by the Military Government, wide-ranging powers to disqualify any political aspirant whose action was 'likely to disrupt the process of grassroots democracy'. The law was amended with Decree 6 of 1992, which widened these powers by absolving the NEC of the duty of explaining or giving reasons for disqualification. This law enabled the NEC to disqualify thirty-two aspirants who had already won their party's nominations for the Senatorial and House of Assembly elections in July 1992. In October 1992, the government sacked elected party leaders and appointed caretaker committees to run their affairs. The caretaker committees were directed by the NEC to re-register party members with the provision that they should not accept more than 2.000 members in each ward (*Tell*, 18/1/1993). The level of arbitrariness in the actions of the NEC was indeed scandalous. True, the elections for gubernatorial positions and state and national assemblies took place, but as we have seen earlier, the presidential election was annulled midway through the counting process.

In November 1993, General Sani Abacha, a leading member of the Babangida administration, took over power in a coup d'état. That move finalised a process began a few months earlier when Babangida was forced to step aside and an interim administration, without either the mandate of the bullet or the ballot, was put in place. The Abacha administration took the hidden agenda to its logical conclusion — the perpetuation of military rule by other means. Given the considerable pressure against the continuation of military rule that followed the annulment of the June 12 presidential election, the Abacha administration was obliged to convene a Constitutional Conference in mid-1994. In December 1994, the Conference resolved that the military should hand over power to a democratically elected government in January 1996. Immediately after the announcement, the regime became very hostile towards the Conference and even prevented it sitting for some months, until the Conference understood that the Abacha regime would not tolerate any challenge to its longevity. Eventually, the Conference promised to review its decision and it was allowed to reconvene and announce a new hand-over date of 1 October 1998, thus giving the regime an initial life span of five years, exactly as Babangida had done. Then the process of political engineering was intensified.

A return to multipartyism was allowed but all the parties that had a real base in the country were refused registration. The five parties that were registered were all led by people who were close friends, allies or proxies of the military regime. Not surprisingly, although they claimed to be politicians seeking political power, most of them were unabashed advocates of the continuation of military rule. In January 1996, an All-Nigeria Summit of Politicians was convened by more serious politicians in Lagos to make collective inter-party plans to guarantee a successful transition. The meeting was broken-up by thugs suspected to be security agents. In the March 1996

non-party local government elections, all candidates perceived to be actual or potential anti-Abacha elements were disqualified from the contest by the National Electoral Commission. The same thing happened in the March 1997 local government elections and the December 1997 state legislative elections. In fact, some contestants were disqualified after they had been duly elected. Government ministers were informally allocated political parties to monitor. With the parties under control, a campaign for the prolongation of Abacha's rule was then set in motion.

Organisations calling for the continuation of Abacha's rule started springing up, the most active of which was 'Youths Earnestly Ask for Abacha' (YEAA). On 3 and 4 March 1998, YEAA organised a 'two million man' rally in Abuja to support Abacha's stay in office. Although the government gave 500 million Naira ($5.5 million) for it, only about 100,000 people turned up to the rally (*Africa Confidential*, vol. 7, no. 3, April 1998). Attempts by opposition groups to organise counter rallies were prevented by the security services and those that held rallies without permission were attacked by armed security men. On 15 April for example, police shot and killed three people at an anti-Abacha rally in Ibadan. On 14 May, Wada Nas, one of Abacha's advisers announced that the General would not resign from the army to contest any election, but that he would do so as a serving General.

General Abacha's transition to civilian rule programme was even more farcical than the one under Babangida. Justice Mamman Nasir, Chairman of the Transition Implementation Committee (TIC) openly declared that 'The five registered political parties are owned by the government and not their members. The same government sets agenda for them in terms of manifesto and guidelines and also finances them' (*Nigeria.Com* 9/12/1997). Massive pressure was put on all political parties to nominate Abacha as their presidential candidate. On 16 April 1998, the UNCP, the party with the largest number of seats, declared Abacha as its presidential candidate, although he was not a party member and had not officially asked to be nominated. Immediately after the UNCP nomination, the Government ordered the other parties to nominate their candidates by the nineteenth, giving them just three days each to organise their party conventions. The Grassroots Democratic Movement (GDM) however, allowed other candidates to contest for the party ticket. The main contender was M. D. Yusuf, who was systematically refused security permits to hold meetings and rallies. At the Maiduguri Convention of 19 April, Abacha was declared winner of the nomination over Yusuf with 1,368 to 408 votes, after the police had been called in 'to restore order' and the Chairman of the Convention Committee, Alhaji Isiaku Ibrahim, had resigned in protest. The following day, the Transition Implementation Committee announced that an election would no longer be necessary since all the parties had opted for Abacha. The Electoral Committee instead was simply to organise a plebiscite to confirm Abacha as 'elected President'.

Abacha died or was killed on 8 June 1998. It is irrelevant whether his death was natural or not[10]. What is important for democratic transition in Nigeria throughout the period of Abacha's state terrorism is that people continued to resist his repression, albeit at very high cost to themselves. The human rights community (Campaign for Democracy [CD], Democratic Alternative [DA], Civil Liberties Organisation [CLO], Constitutional Rights Project [CRP], Committee for the Defence of Human Rights [CDHR], National Democratic Coalition [NADECO], United Action for Democracy [UAD], Movement for the Survival of the Ogoni People [MOSOP], Network for Justice and others), continued their struggle for democracy in Nigeria. In March 1998, the National Democratic Coalition and the United Democratic Front formed the Joint Action Commission (JACOM) to 'co-ordinate and implement actions that would advance the demise of Abacha's dictatorship, and return full democratic rule to Nigeria' (*JACOM Press Release* 7/3/1998). The political class, which for so long had been playing the opportunistic role of 'nice and obedient fellows', in order that the military would allow them to return to power, finally realised it was a self-destructive strategy and started challenging Abacha. In April 1998 for example, eighteen leading Northern politicians, 'The G18', under the leadership of Solomon Lar, openly and severely criticised Abacha's plans for self-succession. A week later, leading politicians from the East, the Eastern Mandate Union, under the leadership of former Second Republic Vice President, Alex Ekwueme declared that the 'Self-succession agenda' was 'immoral, unethical, politically unjust and capable of tearing the nation apart. The present transition programme is fatally flawed, illegitimate, fraudulent and incapable of ushering a new era of genuine democratic governance in Nigeria' (*Post Express* 7/4/1998).

The two groups coalesced into the Group of 34 (G 34). This grouping represented a powerful coalition that gave the lie to Abacha's claim that the only opposition to him was from Yorubas from the South West. University lecturers from the North and Northern radicals such as Usman Bugaje (who was also part of the G 18) of the Network for Justice also came in to attack Abacha's self-succession plans. The struggle for democratic transition had become unstoppable in Nigeria. General Abubakar realised it and arranged for a genuine transition to civil democratic rule. On 29 May 1999, General Olusegun Obasanjo was sworn in as elected president of Nigeria's Fourth Republic.

4

Sierra Leone

Introduction

Sierra Leone received its independence from Britain in April 1961 under the leadership of Milton Margai and his Sierra Leone People's Party (SLPP). From the First Republic, the question of military intervention negating political choice has been posed in an acute manner in the country. In the March 1967 General Elections, Siaka Stevens of the opposition All People's Congress (APC) won the polls and he was called upon by the Governor-General to form the government. Brigadier David Lansana, however, staged a coup to prevent political alternation and Siaka Stevens fled to Guinea in exile. The Nigerian military did not invent the annulment of elections. Two days later, junior officers staged a counter coup and declared Siaka Stevens winner of the elections after an inquiry but they did not hand over power to him. On 18 April 1968, warrant officers and other ranks of the army staged another coup and invited Siaka Stevens to come and assume office. In 1971, there was a very bloody attempted coup by Brigadier J. Bangura in which many people were killed, including the coup leader. Since that period, political violence has been a central feature of the political life of Sierra Leone.

Militarism and State Character

In 1978, Siaka Stevens declared a state of emergency and turned Sierra Leone into a one-party state. This move made formal and open opposition to the regime impossible. At the same time, the level of corruption of the regime became very high and its unpopularity skyrocketed. Although Stevens had promised to resign after the 1981 elections, he did not do so until 1986. When he finally stepped down, he refused to hand over to the incumbent Vice President, Ibrahim Koroma as the constitution stipulated. Instead, he brought Major General Saidu Momoh into office. As the new Head of State, Momoh was even more inept than his predecessor and opposition to the regime grew. 'Beleaguered by a crumbling economy, a divided party and attacks from different angles, the Momoh regime conceded to multi-party politics and elections in 1991. As the elections drew near, there were indications that the government intended to rig the elections' (Rashid 1997:38).

It was in this context that the Revolutionary United Front (RUF) led by Corporal Foday Sankoh attacked Sierra Leone from Liberia with the support of Liberian leader Charles Taylor in May 1991. The origins of RUF have been traced to the Freetown-based lumpen culture of 'rarray boys' from where recruits for a 'popular army' were drawn and sent to Libya for training (Abdullah and Muana 1998:177). General Momoh despatched a dispirited and poorly trained and equipped army to combat Sankoh's RUF. It was not an easy task as the RUF were not holding on to territory, but instead adopted guerrilla tactics. On 29 April 1992, General Momoh was overthrown by a group of young, unpaid and disgruntled solders under the leadership of Captain Valentine Strasser who established the National Provisional Ruling Council (NPRC) as the ruling organ. Most of the new leaders were very young, in their early twenties. The new military leaders benefited from the limited opposition that was offered by a rather narrowly based civil society.

Civil Society

The struggle against the steady rise of state repression and democratic regression in Sierra Leone between 1977 and 1992 was led by a small section of civil society composed mainly of students and elements of the lumpen proletariat (Rashid 1997). One of the high points in that struggle was in January 1977 when there were rumours that President Stevens had stolen $40 million from the state treasury. While reading his speech at the convocation ceremony at the university, the students' union organised a demonstration. The government responded by arresting student leaders and organising its own counter-demonstration with the help of young party thugs. Student protests continued however, and government action led to the death of forty students in Freetown. A state of emergency was declared in the country (Rashid 1997:28-29). Resistance by students continued and Siaka Stevens was forced to concede to the organisation of general elections in June 1977.

The 1977 elections were conducted with the state of emergency still in force and the APC government used its incumbency to bulldoze its way into 'stealing the verdict and mandate'. The elections were held 'amid widespread violence, harassment, killing and destruction of rural settlements' (Rashid 1977:29). The opposition SLPP could not organise effective resistance to the state-sanctioned thuggery organised by the APC government, which took most of the seats. The APC was therefore able to perpetuate its rule on the basis of state terrorism. In consecration of that status, the APC organised a fraudulent referendum in 1978 that enabled it to impose one party rule. From the late 1970s to the early 1990s, generations of students and informal lumpen networks established politically active organisations that were able to establish links with the radical press and with the unions in the struggle against the regime (Rashid 1997:37).

When the Momoh regime was overthrown on 29th April 1992, the national radio played non-stop rap and reggae music all day, in fitting tribute to the rise of lumpen culture. 'Lumpen youth also rallied in support of the regime. In an explosion of civic pride and "revolutionary zeal", they cleaned the city, painted murals and images everywhere, repaired pavements and filled potholes' (Rashid 1997:39).

The students and lumpen youth were able to create a culture of resistance to corrupt and authoritarian rule in Sierra Leone. The base of the resistance was however too narrow to be effective in challenging the usurpers of state power. In addition, the construction of a stable democratic polity was undermined by that very culture, with its roots in lumpen circles and behaviour. In fact, although many of the radical youth leaders were incorporated into the regime, the Strasser-led NPRC did not significantly differ from the one it overthrew.

The Culture of Lumpen Violence and the Problematic of Democratic Transition

The pattern of politics in Sierra Leone has tended to repeat itself. In 1967 Siaka Stevens won the Sierra Leonean general elections but was prevented from taking over power by a military coup. Two months before the March 1996 elections were to take place, a coup occurred under the leadership of Strasser who seemed very reluctant to allow a popular vote. Then Captain Strasser was replaced at the apex of the state by Julius Bio, in a palace coup. Bio argued that Strasser was trying to perpetuate his rule. Bio himself started procrastinating on the issue of democracy, on the grounds that the war would not allow free and fair elections. He was however forced to hold the elections in 1996 and a civilian government under Tejan Kabbah assumed office.

The role of alienated lumpen youth has been fundamental in dictating the extremely violent and catastrophic path of Sierra Leoneian politics in the 1990s. The RUF was the organisational expression of that culture. The roots of RUF are in the capital, Freetown. It is here that the rebellious youth culture of the 'Rarray boys' had been breeding since the 1940s. It was a culture that was organised around marijuana, hustling and petty theft, and underwent further expansion and politicisation in the 1970s (Abdullah 1997:51). The drug culture spread from a narrow group of street urchins to more middle class youth and students. Gradually, lumpen culture was elevated and transformed into a site of political socialisation and counter-cultural activities, with reggae music as a kind of badge of identity. Precisely because the RUF was lumpen in its membership and orientation, it was not able to develop a true revolutionary character, and its actions degenerated into profoundly anti-people manifestations (Abdullah 1997:51).

There has been a strong regional dimension in the development of the culture of violence. Libya was responsible for the initial training and arming of the founders of the RUF in camps in Benghazi in the late 1980s (Abdullah 1997:66). The development and growth of the Sierra Leonean civil war was closely tied to that of Liberia because there was a pact of mutual support between Charles Taylor and Foday Sankoh established as far back as 1989 (Abdullah 1997:67). In fact, some of the Sierra Leonean combatants fought on the side of Taylor. A number of radical students who had been expelled from Sierra Leone went to Ghana to complete their studies and from there were able to link up with others who were in Libya.

A Peace Agreement was signed on 30 November 1996 between President Tejan Kabbah and Corporal Foday Sankoh of the RUF. But the rebel leader was unable to get his forces to abide by the agreement. Sonkoh was finally incarcerated in Nigeria shortly after the accord. The peace accord that was signed turned out to be very tenuous. Most of the parties involved, except President Tejan Kabbah, were not interested in peace. They were making a lot of money from the country's diamond mines and from looting the civilian population. The peace accord merely bestowed an additional political advantage on them, because it led to the official recognition of the RUF. The rebels obtained a role in the new army that was to be constituted, in the new electoral commission, and they also were given immunity from persecution (Bangura 1997). The concessions to the rebels, however, did not guarantee peace.

On 25 May 1997, a rag-tag group of soldiers marched into Freetown, chasing out the legitimate elected regime of Tejan Kabbah. The determined effort of the people of Sierra Leone to elect a government of their choice had once again been frustrated. The putschists released a jailed coup plotter, Major Paul Koroma, and installed him as leader of the Armed Forces Ruling Council (AFRC), the new ruling organ. The putschists called on the RUF to join them and declared Foday Sankoh, then in detention in Nigeria, to be their deputy chair. Some regular Sierra Leoneian soldiers were involved in the putsch. These 'sobels' — soldiers by day and rebels by night — had become a basic feature of the collapsed state in Sierra Leone. Apart from the 'sobels', many soldiers (20 percent by official 1994 estimates), went beyond this straddling and were in full time banditry (Gberie 1997:150). The coup led to massive killing, widespread rape, torture, looting and arson leading to over 400,000 people fleeing the country. The war that had started in March 1991 has led to the displacement of half of the country's population and resulted in at least 30,000 deaths (Abdullahi and Muana 1997:172).

The Sierra Leonean civil war introduced a very high level of lumpen violence into the society. Everyone was affected. Body mutilation, especially the cutting-off of hands, became a very widespread practice at the hands of the RUF rebels[11]. The result of this conflict was in effect one of state collapse. 'It wasn't just that there was a rebellion or violent and bloody usurpation of power (the bloodiest in the country's history). The formal state structures, authority, not to mention law and political order had collapsed' (Gberie 1997:153). The Treasury and Central Bank were burnt down and looted by soldiers representing the new 'authorities'. Soldiers paraded the streets and gunned down a significant part of the elite including politicians, magistrates and journalists.

The government of Tejan Kabbah was restored in March 1998 through the intervention of soldiers sent to Sierra Leone by the Economic Community of West African States Monitoring Group (ECOMOG). A majority of the ECOMOG fighters were Nigerians. While General Abacha was not willing to allow democracy in Nigeria, he devoted a significant part of Nigeria's resources to the re-instatement of constituted authority in Sierra Leone. But the presence of ECOMOG in Sierra Leone was not enough to guarantee peace.

On 6 January 1999, RUF rebels and elements of the former military invaded Freetown for the second time in less than two years. They killed over 6,000 civilians in the capital and abducted thousands of young men and women (Bangura 1999:1). It was a terrible blow for democracy in Sierra Leone. ECOMOG intervened yet again and the Kabbah regime was forced to accept a compromise agreement with RUF. In the Lomé Agreement of 7 July 1999, the RUF were offered eight ministerial posts including the number two post, and absolute immunity for all the crimes committed against the people of Sierra Leone in return for peace. The RUF leader, Foday Sankoh, was even given control of mineral rights, seemingly in recognition of the fact that the control of diamonds had been central to the activities of the warlords. The control of violence by the rebels imposed its logic over the democratic mandate that the Kabbah regime had received from the people. It was a terrible logic. There are too many warlords; not all of them can be bribed and can continue to resort to the blackmail of resuming the civil war as a means of social, economic and political advancement. Not surprisingly, many of the rebel fighters refused to keep to their promise of accepting disarmament and demobilisation.

The war initiated by the RUF penetrated the whole of Sierra Leonean society. It led to 20,000 deaths and the displacement of over 1.5 million people (Musah 1999:76). It generated a counter-army within the society in the form of over 40,000 Mende youth combatants known as the Kamajors. Children were massively dragged into the war through forced conscription as soldiers and as victims of soldiers. For example:

> In 1995, the Revolutionary United Front has been raiding villages to capture children into its ranks and force them to witness or take part in the torture and execution of their own relatives. Thus outlawed and brutalised, and often fed crack or other drugs, the children have been led to neighbouring villages to repeat the exercise (UNICEF 1996).

The children were therefore inducted into the war by force, intimidation or indoctrination. They have been killed, tortured, brutalised and raped. A traumatised generation that would have problems reconciling itself with democracy has been created. Democratic transitions might occur many times in Sierra Leone. The consolidation of constitutional rule will take a very long time. Sierra Leone has diverged considerably from the Ghanaian model of democratisation that has been pursued by President Jerry Rawlings. It has become much closer to the counter model established by Master-Sergeant Samuel Doe in Liberia.

5

Liberia: The Counter Model

Introduction

Liberia was declared a sovereign state in 1847 and is therefore Africa's oldest Republic. It was established as an American outpost for freed slaves that had been released after the abolition of slavery. It developed as a divided society with the Americo-Liberians who constituted only five per cent of the population composing the local elite. They controlled the polity and the economy while the indigenous population were completely marginalised and indeed despised. The party of the Americo-Liberians — the True Whig Party — held sway over the Liberian people for decades. In the twentieth century alone, William Tubman ruled from 1944 to 1971, and William Tolbert was at the helm of affairs from 1971 to 1980, in which year he was violently overthrown.

Liberia was, above all, a client state of the United States. The economy was dominated by mining companies, rubber plantations, and logging concessions belonging mainly to American multinationals. Liberia mortgaged 8,500 square miles, twenty per cent of the land area, as logging concessions to private companies, while the rubber estates occupied fifteen per cent of the land area. By 1970, two companies alone, Firestone and the Liberian Iron Mining Company, were providing fifty per cent of government revenue (Reno 1998:83-85). The country did not even have its own currency but used the American dollar.

Militarism, Warlords and State Character

If Ghana is the model for democratic transition in Anglophone West Africa, then Liberia is the counter model. Regime change in the Liberia transition has involved violence, war and the force of arms. The construction of legitimate authority has hardly been a matter of serious concern, least of all to the military. Indeed, for most of the past twenty years, the Liberian state has been in a state of collapse, and no institutions have been capable of wielding state power legitimately.

The current crisis of the Liberian state started with the coup d'état of 1980. Master-Sergeant Samuel Doe seized power in 1980 in a bloody coup that ended the control of the Americo-Liberians. The move was welcomed by a large part of the indigenous population who assumed that political participation would henceforth be expanded to include them following the ouster of the former elite. In an inauspicious start, thirteen leading members of the Americo-Liberian ruling oligarchy were executed on the beach. Samuel Doe did not however open up Liberian political space. In fact, he narrowed it. He appointed members from his own Krahn ethnic group into key military and security positions. At the same time, he could not really do without the services of Americo-Liberians, and many of them were appointed into top cabinet and administrative positions in the regime. Doe essentially disarmed the army and delegated security to paramilitary units controlled by his ethnic allies. He got rid of his rivals in the military by accusing them of plotting coups against him. He then concentrated on enriching himself by looting public corporations. The Cold War that characterised the international political situation of that period provided him American protection because of his strong anti-Soviet and anti-Libyan rhetoric. He was, as it were, the good boy of the Americans.

His American backers encouraged him to organise multiparty elections, an idea he accepted in 1984, especially because of the American offer of $400 million to fund the transition. Elections were duly held in 1985, but Doe, who had become exceptionally unpopular, lost the popular vote. He however rigged the results, awarding himself 51 percent of the votes. Days later, his main rival and former Army Chief of Staff, Thomas Quiwonkpa, launched a coup attempt. 'Doe's ferocious response against his former friend led to acts of savage brutality by the Armed Forces of Liberia against the Gio and Mano of Nimba County where, four years later, Taylor found fertile ground for rebel recruitment when his NPFL invaded Liberia' (Sesay 1996:414).

Liberia's chronic ethnic divide was therefore exacerbated by these events. Survivors of the violence in Nimba County formed the National Patriotic Front of Liberia (NPLF) to defend themselves. They regrouped in Libya where they received military training and returned to Liberia to fight. In December 1989, the NPLF fighters under Charles Taylor launched a war with one hundred and fifty troops in Nimba County. They were able gradually to capture most of the country. Since the war started, no functional state has existed in Liberia. Taylor's war was widely welcomed because most of the society had become completely disenchanted with Samuel Doe. Charles Taylor had set out to take over the Executive Mansion in Monrovia, and in a few months he was master of most of the country.

Unable to offer effective resistance to Taylor's fighters, Doe entrenched himself in Monrovia. The then Nigerian President, Ibrahim Babangida, was alarmed at the ease with which a fellow military dictator was being routed by a civilian force and canvassed for an ECOWAS intervention (Ellis 1998:2). The role of Libya as well as the Francophone countries Côte d'Ivoire and Burkina Faso, in supporting Taylor, was also worrying to Nigeria and some other West African countries. The intervention force, ECOMOG, moved into the country in September 1990. It encouraged the establishment of various militias to help fight the NPLF and thereby extended and deepened the atrocities of war in the country. About 200,000 people, eight per cent of the Liberian people, died in the subsequent fighting or were massacred (Reno 1998:79). Samuel Doe himself did not survive. In September 1990, Prince Yomi Johnson, a former Taylor adviser and breakaway warlord, captured Doe, tortured him brutally and killed him, recording every gory detail on a video cassette. The war ended in 1996 following the Abuja Peace Accord. By that time, half of the country's 2.5 million population had been killed, maimed or displaced.

The war was very costly not only for the Liberian people, but also for Nigeria. While welcoming home the last batch of Nigerian troops from Liberia, President Obasanjo revealed that between 1990 and 1997 Nigeria had spent about $8 billion and lost five hundred soldiers in the Liberian civil war. Operation Liberty, as the intervention has been called, was a huge drain on Nigeria's human and financial resources (*Triumph* 26/10/99).

Violence and the Problematic of Democratic Transition

One of the most terrible effects of the Liberian civil war was the multiplication of armed groups and gangs. Samuel Doe had initiated the process by establishing and arming parallel security organisations. The rebel groups themselves displayed very strong fissiparous tendencies. Thus by 1995 there were seven major rebel factions involved in the war (Tokpa 1995:2). All of these groups became heavily involved in commercial pursuits. Indeed, it has been argued that the warlord logic in Liberia was essentially commercial:

> Warlord politics emerged as a result of a social coalition of enterprising strongmen, small-scale foreign commercial operators and a small segment of the country's youth ... (under conditions which) gave strongmen the political and financial autonomy to seek their own fortunes at the expense of a central authority (Reno 1998:80).

These warlords were involved in the gold and diamonds business as well as in various trading networks. They engaged in war in order to further their commercial and business interests. This factor fuelled the war and made peace negotiations difficult. Foreign intervention appeared the only solution.

The arrival of ECOMOG in 1990 however prolonged the Liberian civil war for at least seven more years. As has been cynically argued by Ellis, the end of the war in Liberia and the organisation of elections had little to do with the Liberian people. It was an outcome forged in the battle of powerful forces:

> By 1995 Taylor had come to realise that he would never become president without Nigeria's tolerance, and the Nigerian government had come to see that it could never put an end to its intervention, and the constant drain on lives and on the treasury, without accepting the reality of Taylor's influence. Slowly these two protagonists shaped a deal before the July 1997 elections. Nigeria would allow Taylor to take the presidential seat if he would agree to respect Nigeria's interests. Taylor agreed to cease his hostility to Nigeria and to support Abuja's diplomatic and commercial pretensions in the region. So the current peace was born (Ellis 1998:4)

Thus in July 1997 the notorious warlord Charles Taylor was chosen as president of Liberia in elections that were possibly the most free and fair in the history of the country. In the opinion of most observers, the Liberian people realised that they were obliged to vote for him if peace was to return to the country. Subsequent events have shown how vain this hope was, and the recent removal of Taylor — after intense pressure from African and Western states — once again has opened a window of opportunity for a transition to legitimate authority. But matters are far from settled for the unhappy residents of this war-torn country.

As in Sierra Leone, the chances of democratic consolidation in Liberia have been seriously compromised by the culture of violence that has permeated society. About one quarter of the combatants that fought in the various factions, comprising about 20,000 persons, were children (UNICEF 1996). Some of them were as young as seven years old. A whole generation has been bred in a culture of violence. Too many warlords have developed a stake in war — with a lifestyle of luxury based on looting, raping and lawlessness. While the majority of the Liberian people are committed to democratic consolidation, the entrepreneurial spirit of warlordism might once again crush the lives and hopes of the people.

6

The Gambia

Introduction

The Gambia, as is the case with Ghana, has been one of the African states that has been pursuing structural adjustment programmes since the early 1980s. The country is considered one of the 'good examples' of economic reform by the International Monetary Fund and the World Bank. At the political level, the Gambia was also known as one of the few bastions of liberal democracy in the African continent. The country maintained elected constitutional regimes from independence in 1965 up till the coup d'état of 1994, when a military regime seized power. The new military regime was constrained to arrange a rapid transition programme and organise elections within two years. However, the military leader, Colonel Yahya Jammeh, contested and won the 1996 presidential elections, and is therefore the current elected leader of the country.

Smallness and the Attempt at Confederation

One of the most important political specificities of the Gambia is its geographical and demographic smallness. The question had often been posed, can such a tiny political community develop and sustain a viable democratic state? One response to the perceived problem of smallness has been that of integration into, or federation with, Senegal — an option that has always been an important item on the political agenda. For a very long time 'Senegambia', had been considered an area that begs for federation. The cultures and societies of Senegal and the Gambia dove-tail into each other and they otherwise have much in common. There is a Senegambian social space defined by geography and history. It is characterised by common religious practices, social stratification and vehicular languages that make it distinct from the rest of the West African region (Sall 1992:439-43).

The Gambia is a thin strip of territory on the banks of river Gambia, 'inserted', or so it seems, in the centre of Senegal. The Gambia is a very small territory comprising only 11,300 square kilometres, ten per cent of which is the river. The country's tiny size has therefore been one of the reasons advanced for the necessity of some kind of union with Senegal. Many have doubted that the country was viable as an independent state. For Senegal, the fact that the Gambia split the country into two, and created difficulties of access to the restive Casamance region to the south, was a major problem (Sall and Sallah 1994:117). Senegal has also been concerned with the parallel cross border trade, organised from the Gambia, a flow that has been impossible to control.

The establishment of the Senegambian Confederation was however the result of an attempted coup d'état in the Gambia on 30 July 1981, during which the putschists announced the introduction of a Marxist-Leninist programme.[12] Senegal sent half of its army to quell the putsch on behalf of President Jawara and in an improvised resistance to the 'Senegalese invasion', almost two thousand Gambians were reported killed (Sall 1992:447). Up till that time, the Gambia had been a blissfully peaceful country that did not even maintain an army. Not surprisingly, the popular imagination was marked and traumatised by the strong presence and brutality of an occupying force. The Confederation was therefore established as a security apparatus to maintain Jawara in power and to cater for Senegalese security concerns. Indeed, at that time, there was a lot of political agitation in the Casamance region. Ten days after his re-instatement, President Jawara announced the idea of a confederation with Senegal, while at the same time, President Diouf announced the integration of Senegal and the Gambia with the intention of establishing a single state (Sall 1992:448). The Confederal Pact provided for the merger of the armed and security forces of the two countries, the development of economic and monetary union and the co-ordination of their external relations. The Pact was not subjected to a referendum in Senegal and in the Gambia.

Senegal and the Gambia signed a confederal agreement in November 1981 and the Senegambian Confederation was officially established on 1st February 1982. The Confederal Pact was clearly the imposition of Senegalese hegemony over the Gambia. The President of Senegal was perpetually the President of the Confederation while the Gambian President was perpetually the deputy, who could not act as President, even in the absence of the statutory holder of the office. The texts of the agreements even denied the Gambians the right of secession from the Confederation. As has been argued by Sall (1992:431), the reasons for federation are largely mythical. A large network of Gambians (and others, including Senegalese) depended on the parallel trade for their survival and prosperity. Indeed, a stop to parallel trade would have led to a loss of 25 percent of Gambia's revenue, so it was not a policy decision that furthered the interests of the Gambian people (Hughes 1994:50).

Empirically, smallness was not a major problem because the Gambia had a small civil service of less than 20,000, and given the dependence of most African countries on foreign aid, the smaller the better. Indeed, not federating multiplied the chances of the Gambia obtaining international aid. The Gambian political elite also believe that they could pursue a successful development strategy based on the re-export of goods in the region, and foresaw a future as the Singapore of West Africa (Sall and Sallah 1994:124-128). As Sall and Sallah (1998) have noted,

> In fact, it was precisely during the confederal years, and with the implementation of the liberalisation policies imposed by the IMF and World Bank that the re-export trade started booming to unprecedented levels, thus making the original objective of a monetary and economic union a dimmer prospect.

The Gambian people did not have enough objective reasons to desire federation with Senegal, whatever their leaders wished.13 Even the existence of a common Wolof nation provides only dubious grounds for such a union. Although 40 per cent of the Senegalese population belong to the Wolof ethnic group, only 14 per cent of the Gambian do so (Hughes 1994:40). Jawara was clearly a hostage to the interests of Senegal, and the Gambian people were very upset when foreign embassies moved from Banjul to Dakar (Sallah 1998).

If indeed there is a regional dynamic behind economic and social integration, it rests on a wider base. A federation that also included Guinea Bissau and Mauritania might have had a better chance of survival. Most of the Gambians with whom I discussed the issue believed that in the future a larger federation involving four or five countries might be a sound idea. Even Senegal did not have as much to gain from the Senegambian Confederation as is usually assumed. By its investment in damming the Senegal River, the country no longer needed a federal arrangement in order to undertake this step (Hughes 1994:51). Secondly, the Gambia, conscious of its weakness, had never allowed itself to be used as a base by the fighters in Casamance and is unlikely to do so in the future (Sall and Sallah 1994). Thirdly, the huge expenditure on security and on the confederal bureaucracy was too heavy for the Gambia to bear.

The Senegambian Confederation disintegrated following a demand from the Gambia on 1 August 1989 that the Confederal Pact should be re-negotiated such that the presidency of the Confederation should henceforth be a revolving one (Sall 1992:460). At that time, Senegal had been putting pressure on the Gambia to sign a protocol of monetary and economic union and the Gambians were becoming increasingly concerned about losing their last negotiating strength. Following the request, a crisis developed that led to the complete dissolution of the Confederation and the withdrawal of Senegalese troops by the end of 1989. Senegal at that time was coping with two other serious conflicts, with Mauritania to the north and Guinea Bissau to the south and was unwilling to maintain too many hostile fronts. At the end of the day, the Gambian people were still convinced that their smallness was more of an asset than a liability.

Militarism and State Character

The Gambia is the last country in West Africa to undergo the process of militarisation. At independence, the Gambia became the only African country to take the decision not to establish an army. The decision was taken on purely rational grounds — that the country was almost completely surrounded by Senegal and would be unable to establish an armed force that was sufficiently strong to contain the Senegalese army. It was therefore decided that establishing an army would be a waste of money. Rather, the country had no choice but to depend on diplomacy to solve problems that might arise with its larger neighbour. A small paramilitary field force was however established to maintain internal order. The subsequent development of the Gambian military was very strongly influenced by regional factors. Following the 1981 attempted coup and Confederation with Senegal, the decision was taken (or rather, imposed on the Gambia), to establish the Gambian National Army (GNA) under the tutelage of the Senegalese. The GNA only became an independent force in 1989 after the break-up of the Confederation. Immediately the Gambia was freed from Senegalese tutelage, it opened up its military development to other countries in the sub-region. In 1990, the Gambia contributed 150 troops to the ECOMOG contingent in Liberia. These troops were very disgruntled on their return from Liberia over late payments of ECOMOG allowances. Indeed, mutinies by these troops occurred in 1991 and 1992. Nigeria sent a 179 strong 'Training Assistance Group', under the command of a Brigadier-General to provide both the leadership and training. This step led to considerable rancour among the Gambian officer corps (Yeebo 1995:49). Ghanaian officers and security personnel have also been deeply involved with the training of the GNA.

On 22 July 1994, junior officers of the 800 strong Gambian National Army carried out a bloodless coup d'état, overthrowing Jawara's PPP which had ruled since independence in 1965. During the coup, a US warship was moored off the Gambian coast, waiting to hold exercises with the GNA. President Jawara boarded the ship and asked for military intervention, which was refused by the Americans. They however transported him to Dakar, from where he proceeded to Britain. This time, Senegal was not ready to intervene on Jawara's behalf. Anglophone West Africa came in openly in support of the coup. Ghana, Nigeria and Sierra Leone sent a combined high-powered delegation to Banjul to assure the putschists of their support (Yeebo 1995:55). The coup occurred at a time when the PPP was at the height of its unpopularity, just after demonstrations had occurred against a government policy directive requiring people to pay for using public water taps. There was no real resistance to the coup, especially it was felt that President Jawara had run away.

The junta established an Armed Forces Provisional Ruling Council (AFPRC) to rule the country by decree. The new Head of State, Lt. Yahya Jammeh, in the typical coup tradition in Africa, promoted himself to Captain and promised a new era of freedom, progress, democracy and accountability. However, as has been argued:

> The most obvious possible motivation for the coup was the simple desire on the part of the plotters to seize power in order to gain access to the considerable gains, which accrue from controlling the state and the 'rent-seeking' opportunities that such control includes (Wiseman 1996:920).

As with other young officer coup makers in the region such as Jerry Rawlings of Ghana and Thomas Sankara of Burkina Faso, Lt. Jammeh is credited with some charismatic powers. His father was a famous marabout and medicine man whose credentials were generally recognised in the region. It is assumed that the son has acquired some of the skills of his father. Popular belief was that during the coup his strong immersion in 'Joola magic' enabled the Lieutenant to turn bullets into water or to make them bounce off him (Wiseman 1996:919).

Rather than the new era of freedom and democracy that had been promised, the Jammeh regime started by being very repressive. In November 1994, there were allegations of an attempted coup d'état and the alleged coup leaders were killed. Similarly, in January 1995, allegations of an assassination attempt on Jammeh by some of his colleagues in the AFPRC were made, and the purported perpetrators were jailed, one of them dying in detention. Many military officers and politicians were forced to flee the country. In June 1995, the junta established a secret police, the National Intelligence Agency 'designed to obtain and provide the government with information relating to actions or intentions of persons who may be a threat to state security' (Wiseman 1996:928). The organisation became a major instrument for harassing perceived political opponents. With the NIA, the Gambia made its way into the norm of 'actually existing' police states in West Africa. Typically such states function to cover the trails of their corrupt leaders.

Corruption

In justification of the 1994 coup, Jammeh alleged that the Jawara regime had been engaged in 'rampant and outrageous corruption' and 'random plundering of the country's assets to the benefit of a few people' (Wiseman 1996:919). The numerous Committees of enquiry have indeed demonstrated that a high degree of corruption existed under the Jawara regime. Corruption has not however reduced under the Jammeh Administration according to most observers of the Gambian political scene. In June 1995, the Minister of Finance, Ousman Koro Ceesay, was murdered. There were rumours that he had discovered large-scale corruption and that he had to be eliminated to prevent the information becoming public (Wiseman 1996:30). Jammeh's former spokesman, Captain Jallo, was reported to have escaped with three million dollars, which he had simply gone and collected from the Central Bank. In March 1998, Hamat Bah, a member of Parliament, reported to that body that there was still no transparency in the way in which a twenty thousand barrels a day petroleum facility provided by the Nigerian Government was disposed of (*The Gambia News and Report* 17/3/1998 and *The Observer* 23/3/98). The Government denied the allegation. In January 2000 however, a Swiss company that Jammeh had used to siphon $15 million dollars over three years from the Nigerian oil deal referred to above, took him to court in London over their share of the money. The case revealed that Jammeh had indeed paid the money into his personal Swiss account (*ThisDay*, 14/1/2000). The scam around Nigerian oil was one of the most important acts of corruption by the Jawara regime revealed by a commission of enquiry set up ironically by Jammeh himself. According to an opposition politician, Jammeh had insisted that an individual rather than the Central Bank be given power of attorney regarding the country's Swiss bank accounts. It was further alleged that Jammeh had built a two-million *dalasi* house for his mother. Indeed, as Marie Mendy (1998) declared, the signs of increasing corruption were present on the streets for all to see. More and more, expensive flashy cars are to be seen on the roads.

Civil Society

Civil society in the Gambia has been small and not very active until recently. The media is perhaps the strongest aspect of the country's civil society. The country has a history of a virile, even if technically weak, press. Not long ago, many newspapers were simply cyclostyled. The Gambian press however was however subjected to considerable repression under Jammeh. From the very first month, many journalists were beaten and harassed. In May 1992, the *Daily Observer* became the Gambia's first daily newspaper. In 1994, the Liberian editor of the paper, Kenneth Best, was deported.

FOROYAA (Freedom), the paper of the People's Democratic Organisation for Independence and Socialism (PDOIS), has been one of the most critical organs in the country and a pace-setter in polemics as well as in shaping the nation's political agenda. The paper's editors, Halifa Sallah and Sidia Jatta, refused the offer of cabinet posts from Jammeh and continued with their critical commentaries of the regime. They were charged with and arraigned for illegally publishing a party newspaper (Jammeh had banned political parties), and subsequently convicted. They however continued publishing the paper without the party logo (Wiseman 1996:924). In 1996, the bond paid for publishing newspapers was raised from D1,000 to D100,000. Despite this state pressure, the press has maintained its critical stance.

Citizen FM, an independent radio station, is a good example of the spirit of resistance in the media, and which also had a civic responsibility. It was registered in 1995 as a commercial station. It broadcasts independent news and current affairs programmes in English and local languages. According to the proprietor Baboucar Gaye (1998), six months after launching their news programmes in Wolof and Malinke, the Ministry of Information gave a verbal order to stop them because 'people are taking their anti-government news as the gospel truth'. When Gaye refused to comply, he received a letter from the Ministry of Lands and Local Government asking him to close the station because he had no change of land-use permit for the premises he was using. He explained that he had since applied for the permit and it was up to the Ministry to grant it. Gaye and one of his colleagues were detained in February 1998 for three months for distorting news. On his release from detention, he was charged under the 1913 Telegraph Act for operating a radio without a license.

Other critical elements of civil society are the Gambia Workers Confederation and the Gambia Bar Association. According to Pa Modu Faal, Secretary General of the Gambia Workers Confederation, the Union played a critical role in ensuring that the transition to democracy was successful. He was himself a member of the National Consultative Committee. The unions opposed an attempt to institute a democratic regime without political parties and also insisted that the transition period must be as short as possible.

Gender, Youth and Politics

The long period of PPP rule created a fairly closed governing class in the Gambia composed essentially of elderly male members. But according to Dr

Siga Jagne, Director-General of the Women's Bureau, there has certainly been a change in Gambian political life and the most prominent sign of that change is the marked increase of the younger generation, especially women, in decision-making positions. Most of them are technocrats who are under thirty-five years. Indeed, the Jammeh regime has shown a marked propensity for appointing women into cabinet and there are always four or five women cabinet members. Presently, the Vice President, the Attorney-General and the Education and Tourism ministers are women. This is surprising for a country in which no woman was elected to the current Parliament. One explanation that has been offered is that women are considered less threatening to male office holders (Wiseman 1996:929). This reasoning is however rather frivolous. A new gender policy has been prepared by the Women's Bureau and although it has no affirmative action component, it has elements of gender mainstreaming and policies for enhanced women's access to health-care, education and jobs (Siga Jagne 1998). Amie Joof-Soli (1998), the Chair of the National Women's Council, adds that since Beijing there have been many women's fora which have helped in putting gender issues on the agenda at all levels. There are now two women traditional rulers (Alkalo) in the country. One explanation that has been given was that since the first cabinet was appointed just before Beijing, Jammeh may have highlighted the profile of women to get some recognition as a progressive leader — and so doing also attract foreign aid. In this however he was unsuccessful. 'No money came; instead sanctions rained but the ladies did not lose their jobs and in fact one of them graduated to the number two job' (Editorial, *The Point* 24/9/98). Jammeh therefore deserves some recognition for his relatively progressive gender policy.

As in the other countries reviewed in the region however, Gambian women are still far from emancipation even if some of them are now marching on the corridors of power. As Amie Sillah has argued, 70 percent of Gambian women are poor and 73 percent of them illiterate. At the level of policy, civil service rules still discriminate against female employees with regard to study leave, medical treatment and employment security. In addition, the impact of the Economic Recovery Programme has been devastating for women. Amie Sillah cites the lamentations of a peasant woman in the Gambia:

From sun dawn to dusk, I'm on my feet.

Broken body, clothes tattered and torn.

Muddy drinking water.

Have to travel a distance of two kilometres to get water from a deep well.

I have to wake up very early because of the queue of women at the wells....

Yes, Government talks about girls' education, when is it going to be realised.

I have two boys and two girls in school.

When the going gets tough, I think of taking my girl children out of school.

(International Women's Day article by Amie Sillah, *FOROYAA*, 12/3/1998).

However the Gambia has not been afflicted by the First Lady syndrome. It appears that Jammeh has not allowed his wife (or wives) to play a prominent role.

Elections Without Choice

During the Jawara era, one of the tactics the PPP used to control the electoral system was to make it difficult for many people to contest electoral posts. Candidates were required to resign their jobs to in order to stand for election. For opposition parties such as the PDOIS therefore, the most important aspect of democratic transition was electoral reform (Sallah 1998). In the 1970 Constitution, the Permanent Secretary of the Ministry of Local Government was the returning officer for elections. All sorts of irregularities aimed at helping the incumbents were practised. The government for example refused to use indelible ink to mark voters to promote multiple voting by their supporters. Multiple registrations occurred regularly.

In the transition process therefore, much effort was made to correct problems in the electoral machinery in the new statutes. Indeed, the new 1997 Gambian Constitution can be praised on some scores. As has been stated by President Jammeh himself:

It enfranchises the younger generation between the ages of eighteen and twenty-one, provides for the rights of women, children and the disabled and establishes an Independent Electoral Commission. It prohibits tribalism and other forms of sectarianism in politics (Presidential Address to Parliament, 16 January 1997).

It is indeed a much better Constitution than that in force during the First Republic, contends Sallah (1998). The President can no longer dissolve the National Assembly and remain in power, as was the case previously. The National Assembly can however initiate proceedings to remove the President, an impeachment process which can be confirmed through a referendum. The National Assembly can also establish judicial commissions of inquiry and censure and remove ministers for corruption. Local governments have been made autonomous and councillors are to be elected. Even chiefs and village heads (Alkalo) are to be elected democratically. The Constitution provides for a right of recall of members of parliament. The judiciary, the electoral commission and the auditor general have independent budgets that go directly to parliament. The auditor-general also has enormous powers for checking and approving financial records.

According to Ousainu Darboe, Secretary General of the United Democratic Party (UDP), the strongest opposition party, the new Constitution is indeed better than the old one because of the presence of an Independent Electoral Commission and the fact that the President can no longer unilaterally declare a state of emergency. He however argues that the practice of the rule of law has deteriorated and the harassment of the media has been on the increase. Darboe recalls that the opposition parties have been refused the right to call meetings even in private residences. Members of the security services have also brutalised opposition party leaders and members with impunity. Gambians now realise that they have 'changed a good horse for a bad donkey' concludes Darboe.

Be that as it may, there is very clearly an improved level of debate and activism at the national assembly. The Parliament has questioned several ministers and is no longer just a rubber stamp for the executive. The real question that arises is that during the First Republic, the only choice Gambians enjoyed at election time was Jawara. Is the pattern to be repeated under Jammeh?

The Problematic of Democratic Transition

The Gambia has the privileged position of being one of Africa's oldest democracies. For thirty years, a liberal regime operated. Opposition parties were allowed to compete, relatively free and fair elections took place, and the press was also quite free. Although the Gambia experienced this long period of apparently peaceful liberal democratic rule, democracy never put down strong roots. Dauda Jawara remained the boss of the country from 1962 to the 1994 coup d'état. In fact, the Gambia's ruling party, the PPP, emerged as the leading political force in the country in 1959 when Jawara succeeded in displacing older urban based parties by mobilising the rural population. The ruling party however co-opted most of the leading politicians of the opposition by offering them ministerial posts. The country was a de facto one-party state, although political parties were not banned. Their leaders were simply absorbed into the ruling party. When Cherif Cisse for example left the PPP and established the Peoples Progressive Alliance, he was allowed to lose in the elections and was then offered the post of Governor of the Central Bank and later became a minister. The youth were essentially excluded from the patronage system of the party. Apart from patronage, the PPP also enjoyed the support of local traditional chiefs.

The form of democracy practised in the Gambia was of the Westminister type. Government ministers were chosen from among the members of Parliament. The legislature had virtually no autonomy from the executive and acted as a rubber stamp for government policy. Parliamentarians accordingly all behaved themselves, hoping and praying for the day they might be appointed to office, argues Halifa Sallah, one of the Gambia's leading opposition politicians. The few that tried to revolt were offered posts that shut them up. It could be said that the Gambia's democratic system displayed many flaws; but it was certainly a more competitive and liberal one than others in the region.

On taking over power, the Jammeh junta proposed a transition programme on 24 October 1994. It involved a four-year transition period to democratic rule. There was however an outcry against such a long transition period by the international community and the local political class. In response, an independent National Consultative Committee was established under the chairmanship of a respected surgeon, Dr Lenrie Peters, to consult the people and review the programme. It was composed mainly of lawyers, labour leaders, journalists and youth leaders. They met for two months after which they proposed a two-year transition period, which was accepted by the government.

The transition to democracy in the Gambia has been described by Dr Lenrie Peters (1998) as a partial one. It involved a change from a purely military administration to a combined military/civilian regime. While the Gambia now has a constitutional regime, the fact that Jammeh was able to get himself elected meant he was able to sustain some of the repressive political culture he introduced into Gambian politics.

Alternation of power might not be a realistic expectation in the Gambia at times. According to Baba Jallow (1998), the rural population tends to see those in power as anointed by God. Opposition elements are often seen as jealous people. In addition, the patronage that comes with incumbency increases the material capacity of the regime to generate support. Baba Jallow adds that Jammeh carried out an impressive improvement in the infrastructure of the country, which was widely appreciated. 'Jammeh has done more in three years than Jawara in thirty years' (Jallow 1998). D. A. Jawo (1998) also of the *Observer* newspaper argued that what had changed in the country was that there was less freedom of expression, less openness, less tolerance of opposition and a clear decline in the rule of law and respect for justice. Indeed, Dr Lenrie Peters, the Chair of the National Consultation Committee, declared unequivocally that two years after the 1996 elections, the Gambia was still essentially a military regime with all the previous military decrees on the statute books. The soldiers still patrolled the streets, with intimidating effects.

The consolidation of democracy goes beyond the wishes and plans of individuals, no matter how important they might be at a point in time. What was new in the Gambian situation at the end of the twentieth century was that the people no longer took democracy for granted. They had learnt about the dangers of losing democracy. Various factors suggest that Gambian democracy can enter a mature phase. An articulate opposition, a local intelligentsia and a growing civil society are supportive agents of any enduring regime based upon democratic principles, however imperfect its record may be at any one time.

7

General Conclusion

We have tried to demonstrate that the people of Anglophone West Africa, like other Africans, are in the main highly supportive of the democratic transitions that are once again, as at independence, firmly on the political agenda of the region. Such transitions are not mere facades; properly implemented they respond to the needs of the populations for civic and political rights, freedom of speech, assembly and association as well as the right to vote and be voted for, freedom from arbitrary arrest and the right to fair trial. Attaining these freedoms has not been easy. Too many obstacles have been placed before the people for the process to be considered at all nearing completion even where the basic principle of democratic rule has been conceded.

The most serious obstacle has been that of the military, the security forces and the associated armed gangs that have been able to thwart the people's will. The militarisation of society and the rise of the security state has been the main challenge to democratic transition. It has however reached its limits, and there is a consensus in the region that military rule can only make matters worse. That is the beacon of hope for the future. That the beacon remains dimmed in some cases can in large part be put down to the militarisation of society that has extensively damaged civil society and the institutions of constitutional rule.

Civil society is a part of society that has a life of its own, which is distinct from the state and fairly autonomous from it. According to Shils, the idea of civil society has three main components.

> The first is a part of society comprising a complex of autonomous institutions — economic, religious, intellectual and political — distinguishable from the family, the clan, the locality and the State. The second is a part of society possessing a particular complex of institutions which safeguard the separation of State and civil society and maintain effective ties between them. The third is a widespread pattern of refined civil manners (Shils 1991:4).

This third aspect has not been much emphasised in the current literature on civil society. For civil society to exist, the conduct of members of society towards each other must be characterised by civility. Polished and refined manners are expressions of respect for other members of society. It is a pre-condition for democratic practice as citizenship cannot be effective if the rights and the dignity of the person are not respected. Part of the West African tragedy is that these same 'refined and civil manners', which are essential elements of socialisation in most traditional societies', have been eroded by state terrorism, war and the parochial politics of authoritarian leaders. Citizenship, it should be recalled, cannot be exercised in situations of war and terrorism (Leca 1986:175). The civil aspect of West African society must be rediscovered and re-introduced in the socialisation process.

For a democratic future for the African people, the crafting of democratic institutions must be given a prominent place on the continent's agenda. Anglophone West Africa has suffered excessively from state arbitrariness and violence. Civil society has been infected by the same phenomena. The first phase of democratic transition consists of building peace and tolerance. Education in general and civic education in particular must be given a major role in reconstituting West African society. A central aspect of civic education must be oriented towards the rehabilitation of the concept of politics and liberal democracy. As a result of recent history, popular conceptions about the politics of liberal democracy are all too often that it is a process of thuggery, violence and electoral fraud. It is the image that Chinua Achebe has drawn attention to in his *A Man of the People*. It is the image of dirty politics that Siaka Stevens first established in Sierra Leone or that Samuel Doe established with the 1985 elections. That conception of politics must be combated. We are reminded by Bernard Crick (1964:15), that there is an alternative conception of politics as a great and civilising activity. Politics could be practised as:

> The activity by which different interests within a given unit of rule are conciliated by giving them a share in power in proportion to their importance to the welfare and survival of the whole community (Crick 1964:21).

Stable democracy is rule without state violence; it embraces the values of tolerance and conciliation. That is the message that must be passed on to the people. Democracy is not about Western values as so many authors claim today. It is about tolerance, it is about co-existence in diversity. It is an urgent solution for current problems. It is a universal objective for humanity as a whole. What is clear is that in West Africa there are numerous social actors who share this conception and who have struggled vigorously to promote it.

The Nigerian example is instructive (Ibrahim 1997). Any study of its recent turmoil reveals that a wide spectrum of actors — labour unions, university students, professional associations, women's organisations, intellectuals and journalists — have been very active in the democratic struggle. As Bjorn Beckman has argued, in very arbitrary and authoritarian systems many groups suffer from relations of domination in their social and professional fields and feel obliged to contest them, thereby contributing to the expansion of democratic space:

> The Nigerian experience of the past decade suggests that the agenda of interest groups can be closely linked to broader popular concerns, relating both to democratisation and welfare. Even special and elitist organisations such as university lecturers and students may be seen as giving voice to popular aspirations (Beckman 1997:34).

In addition to specific interest groups, a large number of organisations, movements and alliances specifically devoted to struggles for enhancing democracy and human rights have been formed. The social actors for the construction of democracy therefore exist widely in West African civil society. Some issues have been more or less resolved. Authoritarianism has failed in its promise to build the nation-state and develop the economy. The military has failed in its promise of imposing order and fighting corruption. The military has also lost its manipulative capacity of pretending to be working for the good of the people. The concentration of power in one party or one absolute president has failed to produce hegemony. In the long run, the struggles of the people for democratic transition cannot but bear fruits.

Interviews

I visited Ghana from 15 to 22 March 1998 and interviewed the following:

Professor Joseph Ayee, Head, Department of Political Science, Legon.

Professor E. Gyimah-Boadi, Lecturer, Department of Political Science, Legon.Dr Kwesi Jonah, Lecturer, Department of Political Science, Legon.

Dr Kwame Karikari, Director, School of Communication Studies, Legon.

Dr Yao Graham, Deputy Director, Integrated Social Development Centre and Co-ordinator, Third World Forum, Ghana.

Dr Emmanuel Akwetey, Lecturer, Department of Political Science, University of Stockholm.

Dr Amos Anyimadu, Lecturer, Department of Political Science, Legon.

Felix Anebo. Lecturer, Department of Political Science, Legon.

Chris Atim, General Secretary of the June 4th Movement, member of the PNDC and co-ordinator of the defence committees, and who was also one of the first to go in exile in December 1982 — interview in Dakar, 11 November 1998.

I visited The Gambia from the 23 to the 28 of March 1998 and interviewed the following:

Dr Lenrie Peters who chaired the National Consultation Committee.

Gabriel Roberts of the Independent Electoral Committee.

Halifa Sallah of *FOROYAA* newspaper and an opposition political party activist.

Marie Mendy, civil servant.

Baba Jallow, member of National Consultation Committee and journalist with the *Observer*.

D. A. Jawo of the *Observer* newspaper.

Baboucar Gaye of Citizen FM Radio.

Ousainou Darboe, leader of the United Democratic Party.

Dr Siga Jagne, Director-General of the Women's Bureau.

Amie Joof-Soli, Chair of the National Women's Council.

Pa Modu Faal, secretary-general of the Gambia Workers Confederation.

Usman Sillah, Research Assistant.

Notes

1. The same cannot be said of the Francophone zone where France has made the defence of the French language and 'La Francophonie' a fundamental political issue and indeed, a central aspect of its foreign policy.

2. As we shall see in the Liberian case, Doe organised elections in 1985 but there was a consensus that they were massively rigged and in any case, he could not even maintain a facade of democratisation and civilianisation.

3. Hilary Clinton represents one of the most positive visages of femocracy. She is known to have been playing an active role in policy formulation in her husband's presidency. Although there has been some political opposition to this role, it has been generally accepted as positive because she is known to be very intelligent, articulate and committed to social projects. Enlightened opinion suggests that but for gender bias, she, not Bill, should have been the presidential candidate.

4. When Rawlings and his wife came to power, they met the National Council on Women and Development (NCWD), which had been established in 1975 to serve as the government machinery to advance the interests of women in all spheres of development. Nana Rawlings therefore had to set up her own machinery which was to eclipse the NCWD.

5. Under the Babangida Administration, the Head of State had arrogated to himself, through decree, the status of chief accounting officer of the Central Bank so as to facilitate limitless theft of state funds.

6. Maybe we should use the concept of first wife, since it is generally known that Obasanjo has many wives, out of which he has chosen Stella Obasanjo, née Abebe, to be his 'official wife'.

7. It is very comforting that unlike the other First Ladies, she is going through the due process of formally and properly registering.

8. During the First Republic, there were about 150 parties in the country but only about 10 were politically significant. The party system of the First Republic was much more democratic than what we now have in the Fourth Republic.

9. It was political farce at its worst. Nigeria ran out of photographic materials and Polaroid films in the stampede to produce photographs of their members and emergency imports had to be made and people were paid to have their photographs taken etc. The parties had to hire lorries to carry hundreds of thousands of the hurriedly prepared membership files to the NEC.

10. Since his death, a massive literature proposing various conspiracy theories on how he was killed have emerged. Very likely, most of them are fictional. What is interesting about them, however, is that a wide cross section of Nigerians seemed to believe that Abacha had to die so that Nigeria could survive hence the search for how he was 'killed'.

11. The practice of cutting off the hands of opponents started during the regime of Siaka Stevens but it became widespread during the RUF-led civil war.

12. The attempted coup d'état took place while President Dauda Jawara was attending the marriage of Prince Charles and Lady Diana in London. Jawara was so complacent that he often travelled out of the country for six weeks of vacation to play golf and relax. Many of the coup leaders were Diola, the major group in Casamance, a very frightening situation for the Senegalese.

13. None of the Gambians I interviewed thought that the Senegambian Confederation was a good idea or something that was useful to the country.

Bibliography

General

Adekanye, J. Bayo, 1978, 'On the Theory of Modernising Soldier; A Critique', *Current Research on Peace and Violence*, Vol. III, no.1.

Adekanye, J. Bayo, 1981, *Nigeria in Search of a Stable Civil-Military System*, Westview Press, Boulder.

Adekanye, J. Bayo, 1985, 'The Politics of the Post-Military State in Africa', in Christopher Clapham and George Philip (eds.), *The Political Dilemmas of Military Regimes*, Croomheld, London.

Adekanye, J. Bayo, 1992, 'The Military as a Problem in Comparative Political Analysis', *Nigerian Journal of International Affairs*, Vol. 8, no.1.

Aganbila, G. A., 1993, *Militarisation Among the Ex-British Colonies of West Africa*, PhD Thesis, New York University.

Agbaje, Adigun, 1990, 'In Search of Building Blocks: The State, Civil Society, Voluntary Action and Grassroot Development in Africa, *Africa Quarterly* Vol.30, nos. 3 and 4.

Ake, Claude, 1990, 'The Case for Democracy', *African Governance in the 1990s*, The Carter Center.

Ake, Claude, 1991, *Manchean Dialectics: The State Project and its Decivilizing Mission in Africa*, ISS, The Hague.

Alemika, E. E. O., 1992, *Protection and Realisation of Human Rights in Africa*.

Amin, Samir, 1993, 'History as Iconoclast: A Short Comment', *CODESRIA Bulletin*, no.2.

Amin, Samir, 1990, 'The Issue of Democracy in the Contemporary Third World', Paper for CODESRIA Symposium on Academic Freedom, Research and the Social Responsibility of the Intellectual in Africa, Kampala.

Anyang' Nyong'O, P., 1988, 'Political Instability and the Prospects for Democracy in Africa', *Africa Development*, Vol XXIII, no. 1, pp. 71-86.

Anyang' Nyong'O, P., (ed.) 1987. *Popular Struggles for Democracy in Africa*, Zed, London.

Beckman, B., 1987, 'The Military as Revolutionary Vanguard: A Critique', in Stephen O. Olugbemi (ed.), *Alternative Political Futures for Nigeria*, Nigerian Political Science Association, Lagos.

Beckman, B., 1989, 'Whose Democracy: Bourgeois versus Popular Democracy', *Review of African Political Economy*, no. 45/46.

Beckman, B., 1992, 'Empowerment or Repression? The World Bank and the Politics of Adjustment', in P. Gibbon, Y. Bangura and A. Ofstad (eds.), *Authoritarianism, Democracy and Adjustment. The Politics of Economic Reform in Africa*, Scandinavian Institute of African Studies, Uppsala.

Beckman, B., 1993, 'The Liberation of Civil Society: Neo-Liberal Ideology and Political Theory', *Review of African Political Economy*, no 58.

Chole, E., and Ibrahim, J., (eds.), 1995, *Democratisation Processes in Africa: Problems and Prospects*, CODESRIA, Dakar.

Crick, Bernard, 1964, *In Defence of Politics*, Penguin, Harmondsworth.

Dahl, Robert, 1994, 'A Democratic Dilemma: System Effectiveness versus Citizen Participation', *Political Science Quarterly*, vol 109, no 1.

Dare, L. O., 1991, *The Praetorian Trap: The Problems and Prospects of Military Disengagement*, Inaugural Lecture Series 94, Obafemi Awolowo University Press.

Decalo, Samuel, 1976, *Coups and Army Rule in Africa*, Yale University Press, New Haven.

Diouf, Mamadou, 1998, *Political Liberalisation or Democratic Transition: African Perspectives*, CODESRIA, Dakar.

Finer Samuel E., 1975, *The Man on Horseback: The Role of the Military in Politics*, Harmondsworth, Penguin Books.

First, Ruth, 1975, *The Barrel of a Gun*, Allan Lane, The Penguin Press.

Gutteridge, W.F., 1975, *Military Regimes in Africa*, Metheum, London.

Huntington, Samuel P., 1957, *The Soldier and the State*, Havard University Press, Cambridge.

Huntington, Samuel P., 1968, *Political Order in Changing Societies*, Yale University Press, New Haven.

Hutchful, Eboe, 1989, *Military and Militarism in Africa: A Research Agenda*, CODESRIA Working Paper, no 31, Dakar.

Hutchful, Eboe, 1991, 'Reconstructing Political Space Militarism and Constitutionalism in Africa', in Issa G. Shivji (ed.), *State and Constitutionalism: An African Debate on Democracy*, SAPES, Harare.

Hyden, G. & Bratton, M., 1992, *Governance and Politics in Africa*, Lynne Rienner Publishers, Boulder.

Ibrahim, J., 1995, 'Democratic Transition in Africa: The Challenge of a New Agenda', in E. Chole & J. Ibrahim (eds.), *Democratisation Processes in Africa: Problems and Prospects*, CODESRIA, Dakar.

Ibrahim, J., 1993, 'History as Iconoclast: Left Stardom and the Debate on Democracy', *CODESRIA Bulletin*, no 1, and 'History as Iconoclast: A Rejoinder', *CODESRIA Bulletin*, no 2.

Imam, A. and Ibrahim, J., 1992, 'The Democratisation Process: Problems and Prospects', *Development 1992-3: Journal of SID*.

Kandeh, Jimmy D.,1996, 'What Does the "Militariat" Do When it Rules? Military Regimes: The Gambia, Sierra Leone and Liberia', *Review of African Political Economy*, no 69.

Leca, Jean, 1986, 'Individualisme et citoyennete', in P. Birnbaum and J. Leca (eds.), *Sur L'individualisme*, Presse de la Fondation nationale des sciences politiques, Paris.

Le Vine, Victor, 1997, 'The Fall and Rise of Constitutionalism in West Africa', *Journal of Modern African Studies*, 35 (2).

Pye, Lucian, 1990, 'Political Science and the Crisis of Authoritarianism', *American Political Science Review*, vol. 84, no. 1.

Reno, William, 1998, *Warlord Politics and African States*, Lynne Rienner Publishers, Boulder.

Rudebeck, Lars, 1992 (ed), *When Democracy Makes Sense: Studies in the Democratic Potentials of Third World Popular Movements*, AKUT, Uppsala.

Sage, Alexandra, 1998, 'Première Dames et First Ladies: La Femme du Chef est-elle le Chef du Chef?', *L'Afrique Politique*, Bordeaux.

Shills, Edward, 1991, 'The Virtue of Civil Society', *Government and Opposition*, vol.26, no. 1.

Shivji, Issa, 1989, 'The Pitfalls of the Debate on Democracy' *CODESRIA Bulletin*, vol. XIII no. 4.

Shivji, Issa, 1989, *The Concept of Human Rights in Africa*, CODESRIA, London.

Sithole, M., 1994, 'The Democratisation Process in Africa: Is the Second Wind of Change Any Different From the First', Paper for CODESRIA/Rockefeller Reflections Programme, Dakar.

UNICEF, 1996, *The State of the World's Children*, New York.

Welch, Claude E., (ed.), 1970, *Soldier and State in Africa*, Evanston, Illinois, Northwestern University Press.

Welch, Claude E., 1987, *No Farewell to Arms? Military Disengagement from Politics in Africa and Latin America*, London, Westview Press.

Ghana

Abdul-Wahabi, Gyamila, 1998, 'The 1996 Elections in Ghana: Determinants of Political Choice, A Case Study of the Gukpegu/Sabongida Constituency', Final Year Project, Department of Political Science, University of Legon, Legon.

Adjetey, P. A., 1996, 'The Role of Ghana Bar Association in Ghana's Democratisation Process', in Drah, F. K. and Oquaye, M., (eds.), *Civil Society in Ghana*, Friedrich Ebert, Accra.

Afaril-Gyan, E., 1994, 'Elections and Related Issues During Transition from Military Rule to Civilian Multi-Party System: The Case of Ghana', in O. Omoruyi et al (eds.), *Democratisation in Africa: Volume Two*, Centre for Democratic Studies, Abuja.

Amankwah, K. A., 1996, 'The Role of Pressure Groups — Organised Labour and Other Professional Groups', in Drah, F. K. and Oquaye, M., (eds.), *Civil Society in Ghana*, Friedrich Ebert, Accra.

Amoah, S. A., 1979, *University Students Political Action in Ghana*, Ghana Publishing Corporation, Accra.

Ansah, P. A. V., 1996, *Going to Town*, Ghana Universities Press, Accra.

Anyimadu, Amos, 1997, 'Overdrawing the Nation: The National Question in the Political Theories of Ghanaian Constitutions', in G. Nzongola-Ntalaja and M. C. Lee (eds.), *The State and Democracy in Africa*, African Association of Political Science, Harare.

Assimeng, Max, 1986, 'Rawlings, Charisma and Social Structure', *Universitas*, Legon, 8.

Ayee, Joseph, (ed.),1998, *The 1996 General Elections and Democratic Consolidation in Ghana*, Gold Type, Accra.

Ayee, Joseph, 1997, *Ghana's 1996 General Elections: A Post Mortem*, African Association of Political Science, Harare.

Ayee, Joseph, 1997, 'The December 1996 General Elections in Ghana', *Electoral Studies*, vol 16, no 3.

Ayee, Joseph, 1996, 'The Measurement of Decentralisation: The Ghanaian Experience, 1988-92', *African Affairs*, vol 95.

Badu, Kwasi and Larvie, John, 1996, *Elections 96 in Ghana (Parts 1 & 2)*, Ghana Electoral Commission, Friedrich Ebert, Accra.

Centre for Democracy and Development, 1999, *Popular Attitudes to Democracy in Ghana*, Accra.

Dake, J. M., 1992, *Lamentations of a Patriot: A Political Indictment of J. J.*, Concerned Citizen Platform, Accra.

Drah, F. K., 1993, 'Civil Society and the Transition to Pluralist Democracy, in K. A. Ninsin and F. K. Drah (eds.), *Political Parties and Democracy in Ghana's Fourth Republic*, Woeli Publishing Services, Accra.

Drah, F. K. & Oquaye, M., (eds.), 1996, *Civil Society in Ghana*, Friedrich Ebert Stiftung, Accra.

Dumor, Ernest, 1998, 'Keynote Address: The 1996 General Elections and Democratic Consolidation', in Ayee, Joseph (ed.), 1998, *The 1996 General Elections and Democratic Consolidation in Ghana*, Gold Type, Accra.

Green, D., 1995, 'Ghana's Adjusted Democracy', *Review of African Political Economy*, no.66, vol. 22.

Gyimah-Boadi, E., 1998, 'Instituting Credible Elections in Ghana', in A. Schedler et al (eds.), *The Self Regulating State: Public Accountability in New Democracies*, Lynne Rienner, Boulder..

Gyimah-Boadi, E., 1994, 'Ghana's Uncertain Political Opening', *Journal of Democracy*, vol. 5, no. 2.

Gyimah-Boadi, E.,1997, 'Ghana's Encouraging Elections: The Challenges Ahead', *Journal of Democracy*, vol. 8, no. 2.

Jonah, Kwesi, 1987, 'Social and Economic Conditions for a Stable Democracy in Ghana', in Ninsin, K. & Drah, F. K. (eds.), *The Search for Democracy in Ghana*, Assempa Publishers, Accra.

Katsriku, B. and Oquaye, M., (eds.), 1996, *Government and NGO Relations in Ghana*, Friedrich Ebert, Accra.

Manuh, Takyiwaa, 1993, 'Women, the State and Society under the PNDC', in Gyimah-Boadi (ed.), *Ghana Under PNDC Rule*, CODESRIA, Dakar.

McCarty, Chris, 1997, *Public Opinion in Ghana*, International Foundation for Election Systems, Washington.

New Patriotic Party, 1992, *The Stolen Verdict: Ghana November 1992 Presidential Election.*

Ninsin, Kwame, 1996, *Ghana's Political Transition, 1990-1993: Selected Documents*, Freedom Publications, Accra.

Ninsin, Kwame, 1993(a), 'Some Problems in Ghana's Transition to Democratic Governance', *Africa Development*, vol. XVIII, no. 2.

Ninsin, K. & Drah, F. K., (eds.), 1993, *Political Parties and Democracy in Ghana's Fourth Republic*, Woeli Publishing Services, Accra.

Ninsin, K. & Drah, F. K., (eds.), 1987, *The Search for Democracy in Ghana*, Assempa Publishers, Accra.

Nyoagbe, J. K., 1996, 'Teacher Activism in Ghana: The Past and Present Scenarios', in Drah, F. K. and Oquaye, M., (eds.) *Civil Society in Ghana*, Friedrich Ebert, Accra.

Okudzeto, Sam, 1996, 'The Role of the Association of Recognised Professional Bodies in the Political Struggles of Ghana', in Drah, F. K. and Oquaye, M., (eds.), *Civil Society in Ghana*, Friedrich Ebert, Accra.

Oquaye, Mike, 1980, *Politics in Ghana: 1972-1979*, Tornado Publications, Accra.

Oquaye, Mike, (ed.), 1995, *Democracy and Conflict Resolution in Ghana*, Gold Type Publications, Accra.

Owusu, Maxwell, 1996, 'Tradition and Transformation: Democracy and the Politics of Popular Power in Ghana', *Journal of Modern African Studies*, vol. 34, no. 2.

Parfitt, T. W., 1995, 'Adjustment for Stabilisation or Growth? Ghana and the Gambia', *Review of African Political Economy*, no. 63, vol. 22.

Sakyi-Addo, Kwaku, 1998, 'Ghana's First Lady', BBC Focus on Africa, April-June.

Sandbrook, R. & Oelbaum, J., 1997, 'Reforming Dysfunctional Institutions Through democratisations? Reflections on Ghana', *Journal of Modern African Studies*, vol 35, no 4., pp. 69-87.

Shillington, Kevin, 1992, *Ghana and the Rawlings Factor*, Macmillan, London.

Tackie, M. A., 1996, 'The Role of Civil Society in the Democratisation Process in Ghana with Particular Reference to Women's Participation in Politics and in Leadership Positions', in Drah, F. K. and Oquaye, M., (eds.), *Civil Society in Ghana*, Friedrich Ebert, Accra.

Tsikata, Dzodzi, 1997, 'Gender Equality and the State in Ghana', in A. Imam, F. Sow and A. Mama (eds.), *Engendering African Social Sciences*, CODESRIA, Dakar.

Tsikata, Dzodzi, 1998, 'The First Lady Syndrome', *Public Agenda*, 19 and 26 January.

Verlet, Martin, 1997, 'Ghana: "l'effet Rawling"', *Afrique Contemporain*, no. 182.

Wiilks, Ivor, 1996, *One Nation: Many Histories: Ghana Past and Present*, Ghana Universities Press, Accra.

Nigeria

Abdulraheem, Tajudeen and Olukoshi, Adebayo O., 1986, 'The Left in Nigerian Politics and the Struggle for Socialism', *Review of African Political Economy*, no. 37, December.

Academic Staff Union of Universities, 1986a, *ASUU and the 1986 Education Crisis in Nigeria*, Zaria.

Adekanye, J. Bayo, 1989, 'The Recruitment Policy: Its Sources and Impact on the Nigerian Military', in P.P. Ekeh and E.E. Osaghae (eds.), *Federal Character and Federalism in Nigeria*, Heinemann, Ibadan.

Agudat T. Akinola, 1986, *The Crisis of Justice*, Eresu Hills Publishers, Akure.

Amadiume, I., 1987, *Male Daughters, Female Husbands*, Zed Books, London.

Ananaba, Wogu, 1969, *The Trade Union Movement in Nigeria*, Hurst, London.

Andrae, G. and Beckman, B., 1991, 'Textile Unions and Industrial Crisis in Nigeria: Labour Structure, Organisation, and Strategies', in I. Brandell (ed.), *Workers in Third World Industrialization*, London, MacMillan.

Andrae, G. and Beckman, B., 1992, 'Labour Regimes and Adjustment in the Nigerian Textile Industry', Paper to Workshop on 'The State, Structural Adjustment and Changing Social and Political Relations in Africa', Scandinavian Institute of African Studies, Uppsala.

Awe, B., 1989, 'Nigerian Women and Development in Retrospect', in J.L. Parpart (ed.), *Women and Development in Africa: Comparative Perspectives*, Dalhousie University.

Awe, B., (ed.), 1992, *Nigerian Women in Historical Perspective*, Sankore/Bookcraft, Ibadan.

Ayu, Iyorchia, 1986, *Essays in Popular Struggle: Fela, Students Patriotism, Nicaraguan Revolution*, Oguta, Zim Pan African Publishers.

Bangura, Y., 1986, 'Structural Adjustment and the Political Question', *Review of African Political Economy*, no 37.

Bangura, Y., 1989, 'Authoritarian Rule and Democracy in Africa: A Theoretical Discourse', *UNRISD Discussion Paper no. 18*.

Bangura, Y., 1993, 'Intellectuals, Economic Reform and Social Change...', Conference Paper, Holland.

Bangura, Y., and Beckman, B., 1993, 'African Workers and Structural Adjustment: A Nigerian Case Study', in A. Olukoshi (ed.), *The Politics of Structural Adjustment in Nigeria*, James Currey, London.

Beckman, B., 1997, 'Interest Groups and the Expansion of Democratic Space', in Jibrin Ibrahim (ed.), *Expanding Democratic Space in Nigeria*, CODESRIA, Dakar.

Beckman, B., and A. Jega, 1994, 'Scholars and Democratic Politics in Nigeria', Paper to Conference on 'Knowledge and Development', organised by the Norwegian Association of Development Research (NFU), Tromsö.

Coleman, J. S., 1965, *Nigeria: Background to Nationalism*, University of California Press, Berkeley.

Dennis, C., 1987, 'Women and the State in Nigeria:the Case of the Federal Military Government', in H Afshar (ed.), *Women, State and Ideology*, Macmillan.

Diamond, L., 1988, 'Nigeria: Pluralism, Statism and the Struggle for Democracy', in Diamond, Linz & Lipset, (eds.), *Democracy in Developing Countries*, Vol. 2, Africa, Lynne Rienner Publishers, Boulder.

Dike, Enwere, 1990, 'Nigeria: The Political Economy of the Buhari Regime', *Nigerian Journal of International Affairs*, Vol.16 no.2.

Dudley, B. J., 1973, *Instability and Political Order: Politics and Crisis in Nigeria*, Ibadan University Press, Ibadan.

Ekwe-Ekwe, Herbert, 1985, 'The Nigerian Plight: Shagari to Buhari', *Third World Quarterly* Vol.7,No.3.

Federal Government of Nigeria, 1975, *The Dawn of A New Era*, Government Printer, Lagos.

Federal Government of Nigeria, 1986, *Government White Paper on the Commission of Inquiry in to the Student Crisis at A.B.U. Zaria*, Federal Government Press, Lagos.

Federal Government of Nigeria, 1987, *Report of the Political Bureau*, Government Printer, Lagos.

Federal Government of Nigeria, 1989, *Decree No.47 Student Union Activities (Control and Regulation)*, Federal Government Press, Lagos.

Hashim, Y., 1987, *State Intervention in Trade Unions: A Nigerian Case Study 1975–1978*, ISS, The Hague.

Ibrahim, Jibrin, 1986, 'The Political Debate and the Struggle for Democracy in Nigeria', *Review of African Political Economy*, no. 32.

Ibrahim, Jibrin, 1988, 'La societé contre le bipartisme', *Politique africaine*, no. 32, December.

Ibrahim, Jibrin, 1989, 'Politics and Religion in Nigeria: The Parameters of the 1987 Crisis in Kaduna State', *Review of African Political Economy*, no. 45/46.

Ibrahim, Jibrin, 1991, 'Le développement de l'État nigerian', In J-F Medard (ed.), *Les États d'Afrique noire: formation, mécanisme et crise*, Karthala, Paris.

Ibrahim, Jibrin, 1991, 'Religion and Political Turbulence in Nigeria', *Journal of Modern African Studies*, no. 29(1).

Ibrahim, Jibrin, 1991, *L'acces à l'État: classes sociales, élites, factions; une étude du 'National Party of Nigeria'*. Ph.D thesis, Bordeaux.

Ibrahim, Jibrin, 1993, 'The Transition to Civil Rule: Sapping Democracy in Nigeria', in A. Olukoshi (ed.), *The Politics of Structural Adjustment in Nigeria*, James Currey, London.

Ibrahim, Jibrin, (ed.), 1997, *The Expansion of Democratic Space in Nigeria*, CODESRIA, Dakar.

Ibrahim, Jibrin, 1997, 'Obstacles to Democratization in Nigeria', in P. A. Beckett and C. Young (eds.), *Dilemmas of Democracy in Nigeria*, University of Rochester Press, Rochester.

Ibrahim, Jibrin, 1997, 'Political Scientists and the Subversion of Democracy in Nigeria', in G. Nzongola-Ntalaja & M. C. Lee (eds.), *The State and Democracy in Africa*, African Association of Political Science, Harare.

Ibrahim, Jibrin, 1997, 'Political Scientists and the Subversion of Democracy in Nigeria', in G. Nzongola-Ntalaja & M. C. Lee (eds.), *The State and Democracy in Africa,,* African Association of Political Science, Harare.

Imam, Ayesha, 1993, 'If You Don't Do These Things For Me I Won't Do Seclusion For You,' PhD Thesis, Sussex.

Jega, A.M., 1988, 'The Labour Movement and Popular Democratic Struggles in Nigeria', Mahmoud Tukur Memorial Symposium, Zaria, November.

Jega, A.M., 1990, 'The Influence of Class Actors in Nigeria's Transition Process', Conference on Democratic Transition and Structural Adjustment, Stanford University, August.

Jega, A.M., 1993, 'Professional Associations and Structural Adjustment', in Olukoshi, A. (ed.), *The Politics of Structural Adjustment in Nigeria*, James Currey, London.

Jega, A. M., 1997, 'Intellectuals and Academics in the Struggle for Democracy', in Ibrahim, Jibrin (ed.), *Expanding Democratic Space in Nigeria*, CODESRIA, Dakar.

Lukham, Robin, 1971, *The Nigerian Military: A Sociological Analysis of Authority and Revolt 1960 – 1967*, Cambridge University Press, Cambridge.

Madunagu, Edwin, 1980, *The Tragedy of the Nigerian Socialist Movement and Other Essays*, Centaur Press, Calabar.

Mba, Nina 'Kaba and Khaki, 1989, 'Women and the Militarised State in Nigeria', in J. Parpart and K Staudt, *Women and the State in Africa*, Lynne Rienner, Boulder and London.

Mama, Amina, 1997, 'Feminism or Femocracy? State Feminism and Democratisation', J. Ibrahim *Expanding Democratic Space in Nigeria*, CODESRIA, Dakar.

Momoh, A., 1992, 'The Philosophical and Ideological Foundations of the Transition to Civil Rule in Nigeria', in B. Caron, A. Gboyega, and E.O. Osaghae (eds.) *Democratic Transitions in Africa*, CREDU, Ibadan.

Momoh, A. and Adejumobi, S., 1999, *The Nigerian Military and the Crisis of Democratic Transition: A Study in the Monopoly of Power*, Civil Liberties Organisation, Lagos.

Muazzam, Ibrahim, 1982, 'The PRP-Imoudu and the Politics of Realignment: A Call to March Separately but Strike Together', Mimeo, Kano.

Naanen, Ben, 1995, 'Oil Producing Minorities and the Restructuring of Nigerian Federalism: The Case of the Ogoni People', *Journal of Commonwealth and Comparative Politics*, vol 33, no 1.

National Consultative Forum on National Conference, 1999, *Agenda for Democracy*, Lagos.

Nnoli, Okwudiba, 1984, 'Musical Chairs and the Cheers For the Music', *Studies in Politics and Society* No. 2, October.

Okeke, Phil, 1998, 'First Lady Syndrome: The (En) Gendering of Bureaucratic Corruption in Nigeria', *CODESRIA Bulletin*, nos 3 & 4.

Olagunju, T & Oyobaire, S, (eds.), 1989, *Foundations of a New Nigeria*, The IBB Era, Precision Press, Lagos.

Olagunju, T. and S. Oyobaire (eds.), 1991, *For Their Tomorrow, We Gave Our Today: Selected Speeches of IBB*, Vol. 2, Sefari Books, St. Helier.

Olukoshi, Adebayo and Abdulraheem, Tajudeen, 1985, 'Nigeria crisis management under the Buhari Administration', *Review of African Political Economy* No.34 December.

Olukoshi, Adebayo, 1991, 'Nigerian Marxist Responses to the Formation of the Nigerian Labour Party (NLP)', in Christian Neugebuer (ed.), *Philosophy, Ideology and Society in Africa*, Peter Lang, Frankfurt.

Olukoshi, Adebayo, 1993, 'The Current Transition from Military Rule in Nigeria', Paper Presented to the Workshop on 'Experiences of Political Liberalization in Africa', Centre for Development. Research, Copenhagen, June 3-4.

Olusanya, Gabriel, 1982, *The West African Student's Union and the Politics of Decolonization 1925-1958*, Ibadan, Daystar Press.

Omu, Fred, 1978, *The Press and Politics in Nigeria: 1880-1937*, Longman, London.

Osoba, Segun, 1993, 'Crisis of Accumulation and Democratic Misadventure in Nigeria: A Retrospective and Prospective Analysis', *Ife Journal of History* Vol.1, No.1, Jan-June.

Othman, S, 1984, 'Classes, Crises and the Coup: The Demise of Shagari's Regime', *African Affairs*, vol 83.

Otobo, Dafe, 1988, State and Industrial Relations in Nigeria,. Malthouse Press, Lagos.

Owolabi, Olayiwola, 1992, 'The Military and Democratic Transition: An Analysis of the Transition Programme of the Babangida Administration', in B. Caron, A. Gboyega and E. Osaghae (eds.), *Democratic Transitions in Africa*, CREDU, Ibadan.

Oyediran, Oyeleye, 1988/89, 'The Gospel of the Second Chance. A Comparison of Obasanjo and Babangida Military Disengagement in Nigeria', *Quarterly Journal of Administration* Vol. XXIII No 1.

Shettima, K. A., 1989, 'Women's Movement and Visions: The Nigeria Labour Congress Women's Wing', *Africa Development* XIV, 3.

Shettima, K.A., 1993, 'Structural Adjustment and the Student Movement in Nigeria', *Review of African Political Economy* No.56.

Shettima, K. A., 1997, 'Students and Youth Vanguardism in the Struggle for Democracy', in Ibrahim, Jibrin (ed.) *Expanding Democratic Space in Nigeria*, CODESRIA, Dakar.

Shettima, K. A., 1995, 'Engendering Nigeria's Third Nigeria's Third Republic', *African Studies Review*, vol. 38, no 3.

Turner, Terisa, 1976, 'Multinational Corporations and the instability of the Nigerian State', *Review of African Political Economy*, no 5.

Turner, Terisa, 1978, 'Commercial Capitalism and the 1975 Coup', in Keith Panterbrick (ed.), *Soldier and Oil: The Political Transformation of Nigeria*, London, Frank Cass.

Ukpabi, C., 1985, *The Origins of the Nigerian Army*, Gaskiya Corporation, Zaria.

Women in Nigeria, 1985, *The WIN Document: Conditions of Women in Nigeria and Policy Recommendations to 2,000 AD*, WIN, Zaria.

Women in Nigeria, 1985, *Women and the Family: Proceedings of the Second Annual WIN Conference*, CODESRIA, Dakar.

Women in Nigeria, 1985, *Women in Nigeria Today*, Zed Press, London.

Ya'u, Y. Z., 1997, 'The Mass Media in the Struggle for Democracy', in Ibrahim, Jibrin (ed.), *Expanding Democratic Space in Nigeria*, CODESRIA, Dakar.

Zasha, J., 1985, 'The State and Trade Unions', *Nigerian Journal of Political Science*, Vol.4, No.1 & II.

Liberia

Ellis, Stephen, 1998, 'Liberia — the Heart of a West African Struggle', *News from Nordiska Afrikainstitutet*, January.

Reno, William, 1998, *Warlord Politics and African States*, Lynne Rienner Publishers, Boulder.

Sesay, Max, 1996, 'Politics and Society in Post-War Liberia', *Journal of Modern African Studies*, vol 34, no 3.

Takpa, Alaric, 1995, 'Class, Ethnicity and the Army in Transitional Liberia: An Analysis of the Interplay of Domestic and Foreign Constraints on the Liberian Crisis', Paper for CODESRIA Eighth General Assembly.

Sierra Leone

Abdullah, I. and Muana, P., 1998, 'The Revolutionary United Front of Sierra Leone', in C. Clapham (ed.), *African Guerrillas*, James Currey, London.

Abdullah, Ibrahim, 1997, 'Bush Path to Destruction: The Origin and Character of the Revolutionary United Front', *Africa Development*, Vol. XXII, Nos 3 & 4.

Abdullah, Ibrahim et al., 1997, 'Lumpen Youth Culture and Political Violence', *Africa Development*, Vol. XXII, Nos 3 & 4.

Abraham, Arthur, 1997, 'War and Transition to Peace: A Study in State Conspiracy in Perpetuating Armed Conflict', *Africa Development*, Vol. XXII, Nos 3 & 4.

Bangura, Yusuf, 1999, 'Strategic Policy Failure and State Fragmentation in Sierra Leone', Binghampton University Conference on Peace Keeping in Africa, Bellagio, June.

Bangura, Yusuf, 1997a, 'Understanding the Political and Cultural Dynamics of the Sierra Leone War: A Critique of Paul Richard's Fighting for the Rain Forest', *Africa Development*, Vol. XXII, Nos 3 & 4.

Bangura, Yusuf, 1997b, 'Reflections on the Abidjan Peace Accord', *Africa Development*, Vol. XXII, Nos 3 & 4.

Fyle, C. M., 1995, 'Conflict and Population Dispersal: The Refugee Crisis in the Mano River Tri-State Area', Paper for Eighth General Assembly, CODESRIA, Dakar.

Gberie, Lansana, 1997, 'The May 25 Coup d'État in Sierra Leone: A Militariat Revolt?,' *Africa Development*, Vol. XXII, Nos 3 & 4.

Muana, Patrick, 1997, 'The Kamajol Militia: Violence, Internal Displacement and the Politics of Counter-Insurgency', *Africa Development*, Vol. XXII, Nos 3 & 4.

Musah, Abdel-Fatau, 2000, 'A Country Under Siege: State Decay and Corporate Military Intervention in Sierra Leone', in A-F Musah and J. K. Fayemi (eds.), *Mercenaries: An African Security Dilemma*, Pluto Press, London.

Rashid, Ishmail, 1997, 'Subaltern Reactions: Lumpens, Students and the Left', *Africa Development*, Vol. XXII, Nos 3 & 4.

Reno, William, 1998, *Warlord Politics and African States*, Lynne Rienner Publishers, Boulder.

The Gambia

African Commission on Human and People's Rights, 1994, *Periodic Report of Gambia*, Banjul.

Article 19, 1994, *Democracy Overturned: Violation of Freedom of Expression in the Gambia*, London.

Diop, M-C., (ed.), 1994, *Le Sénégal et ses voisins*, Société-Espaces-Temps, Dakar.

Fletcher, A. J., 1978, 'Party Politics in the Gambia', PhD Thesis, University of California, Los Angeles.

Government of Gambia, 1995, *Report of the National Consultative Committee on the Armed Forces Provisional Ruling Council's Programme of Rectification and Timetable for Transition to Democratic Constitutional Rule in the Gambia*, Banjul.

Hughes, A., 1994, 'L'éffondrement de la confédération de la Sénégambie', in Diop, M-C (ed.), *Le Sénégal et ses voisins*, Société-Espaces-Temps, Dakar.

Hughes, A., 1991, 'The Attempted Coup d'État of 27 July 1981', in Hughes, A. (ed.), *The Gambia: Studies in Society and Politics*, Birmingham University African Studies Series, Birmingham.

Parfitt, T. W., 1995, 'Adjustment for Stabilisation or Growth? Ghana and the Gambia', *Review of African Political Economy*, no 63, vol 22.

People's Progressive Party, 1992, *The Voice of the People: The Story of the PPP*, Baoueli Publications, Banjul.

Sallah, Tijan, 1990, 'Economics and Politics in the Gambia', *Journal of Modern African Studies*, vol 28, no 4.

Sall, E. and Sallah, H., 1994, 'Senegal and the Gambia: The Politics of Integration', in Diop, M-C (ed.), *Le Sénégal et ses voisins*, Société-Espaces-Temps, Dakar.

Sall, Ebrima, 1995, 'Gambie: Le Coup d'État de juillet 1994', *Afrique politique,* Bordeaux.

Sall, Ebrima, 1992, *Petite dimension et gouvernementalité: Essai d'analyse de l'édification de l'Etat en Gambie*, Thèse, Université de Paris I.

Senghor, J. C., 1979, *Politics and the Functional Strategy to International Integration: Gambia in the Senegambian Integration*, PhD thesis, Yale.

United States State Department, 1997, *The Gambia Country Report on Human Rights*, Washington.

Wiseman, John, 1996, 'Military Rule in the Gambia: an Interim Assessment', *Third World Quarterly*, vol 17, no 5.

Zaya, Yeebo, 1995, *State of Fear in Paradise: The Military Coup in the Gambia and its Implications for Democracy*, ARIB, London.